New Slow Cooker Cookbook for Beginners

1600 Days Succulent & Nutrient-Rich Recipes Book for Evoking The Warmth and Comfort of Slow-Cooking Meals.

Latasha D. Hegarty

CONTENTS

INTRODUCTION

Hey there, fellow food adventurers! Are you ready to embark on a journey of mouthwatering aromas and delectable delights? Look no further, because you're about to discover the culinary wizardry of none other than the Slow Cooker Extraordinaire herself, Latasha D. Hegarty!

Picture this: succulent meats falling off the bone, hearty stews brimming with flavor, and luscious desserts that melt in your mouth. All of this, achieved with just a sprinkle of magic—Latasha's Slow Cooker Cookbook is here to make your taste buds tingle with anticipation!

So, who is this mastermind behind the slow-cooked magic? Well, Latasha is not your average cookbook author. She's the culinary equivalent of a time-traveling sorceress, blending traditional wisdom with contemporary flair. Armed with her trusty slow cooker, she has perfected the art of transforming humble ingredients into culinary masterpieces fit for a feast.

But wait, there's more to Latasha than her exceptional cooking skills. Picture a lively personality, a contagious zest for life, and a pinch of humor that will have you chuckling as you flip through her cookbook's pages. Latasha is not afraid to roll up her sleeves, tie on an apron, and get her hands messy in the pursuit of culinary excellence. Her kitchen is a playground of creativity, and she invites you to join the fun!

From busy professionals to culinary novices and seasoned foodies, Latasha's Slow Cooker Cookbook has something for everyone. Are you a busy bee with limited time for meal prep? Latasha's got your back with time-saving and effortless recipes that taste like you spent hours slaving over the stove.

Or perhaps you're new to the kitchen and feeling a tad bit nervous about cooking? Fear not! Latasha's cookbook will gently guide you through the enchanting world of slow cooking, making you feel like a seasoned chef in no time.

So, my fellow food enthusiasts, fasten your apron strings, dust off that slow cooker, and get ready to embark on a culinary adventure like no other. Latasha D. Hegarty's Slow Cooker Cookbook is your passport to a magical realm of tantalizing flavors and simple yet sensational dishes.

Now, let's dive in and let the slow-cooked enchantment begin! Bon appétit!

What are the benefits of Slow Cooker Cookbook?

Convenience: Slow cookers are ideal for individuals with busy schedules or those who prefer to spend less time in the kitchen. Once the ingredients are added to the pot, the slow cooker takes care of the rest, requiring minimal supervision. It's perfect for preparing meals in advance or when you want to come home to a hot, ready-to-eat dinner.

Retains Moisture: Slow cooking creates a closed environment that traps steam, ensuring that the food retains its moisture and remains tender and flavorful.

Versatility: Slow cookers can prepare a wide range of dishes, including soups, stews, chilis, roasts, casseroles, and even desserts.

Safety: Slow cookers are generally safe to use, as they are designed to operate at low temperatures and are equipped with temperature controls and safety features.

Economical: Slow cookers are energy-efficient because they use a lower wattage compared to traditional ovens or stovetops.

Popular recipes for slow cookers include beef stew, pulled pork, chicken curry, chili, pot roast, and many others. Slow cooking allows tough cuts of meat to become tender and infuses flavors throughout the dish as it cooks slowly.

Who is suitable for Slow Cooker Cookbook?

A Slow Cooker Cookbook is suitable for a wide range of individuals, including:

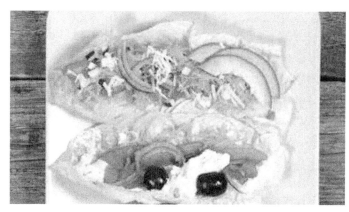

Busy Professionals
People with hectic work schedules who have limited time to cook can benefit from slow cookers. The cookbook offers recipes that allow them to prepare delicious meals with minimal effort and time investment.

Working Parents
Parents juggling work and family responsibilities can find slow cookers invaluable. The cookbook provides family-friendly recipes that can be prepared in advance, making dinner preparation easier during busy evenings.

College Students
College students living in dorms or apartments with limited kitchen facilities can use slow cookers to create simple and budget-friendly meals.

Beginners in the Kitchen
Those who are new to cooking or lack culinary experience can find slow cookers easy to use and a great way to build confidence in the kitchen.

Seniors
Older adults who may prefer easier cooking methods can enjoy the convenience of slow cookers. The cookbook offers recipes that are gentle on their hands and require minimal active cooking.

Health-Conscious Individuals
Slow cookers can be used to prepare healthy meals with lean meats, fresh vegetables, and whole grains. The cookbook provides nutritious recipes that cater to health-conscious individuals.

Those Seeking Convenience
People who value convenience and want to simplify

their meal preparation process will appreciate the slow cooker's set-it-and-forget-it approach.

Meal Preppers
Individuals who like to prepare meals ahead of time can use slow cookers to cook in large batches, which can be portioned and stored for later consumption.

Food Enthusiasts
Even seasoned cooks and food enthusiasts can find inspiration in the cookbook, discovering new flavors and techniques to enhance their culinary repertoire.

Anyone Wanting Delicious Comfort Food
Slow cookers excel at creating comforting and flavorful dishes, making the cookbook suitable for anyone who enjoys hearty and satisfying meals.

Overall, a Slow Cooker Cookbook is designed to accommodate various lifestyles and cooking preferences. It caters to individuals looking for simplicity, convenience, and flavorful meals that require minimal hands-on cooking. Whether you're a busy professional, a cooking novice, or someone who appreciates comforting and delicious food, a slow cooker cookbook can be a valuable addition to your kitchen resources.

What do I need to know about using Slow Cooker Cookbook?

●Follow Recipes Carefully
Slow cooking is a precise method, and ingredients and cooking times are crucial for successful outcomes. Follow the recipes in the cookbook accurately, especially when it comes to liquid measurements and cooking times.

●Choose Appropriate Recipes
Ensure that the cookbook's recipes align with your dietary preferences, restrictions, and cooking skill level. Some cookbooks cater to specific diets, such as vegetarian, vegan, or gluten-free, while others offer a variety of options suitable for different tastes.

●Prepare Ingredients Beforehand
Most slow cooker recipes require some preparation before adding the ingredients to the pot. Chop vegetables, trim meat, and gather all the necessary spices and seasonings ahead of time to make the cooking process smoother.

●Layer Ingredients Wisely
Proper layering of ingredients is essential in slow cooking to ensure even cooking and optimal flavor distribution. Follow the cookbook's instructions on layering, especially when using tougher cuts of meat or root vegetables.

●Be Mindful of Cooking Times
Slow cookers work at low temperatures, so don't expect rapid cooking. Cooking times can vary based on the recipe, ingredient quantity, and your slow cooker's specific settings. Allow sufficient time for the

food to cook thoroughly.

●Use the Right Liquid Amount
Slow cookers need adequate liquid to create steam and prevent the food from drying out. Follow the cookbook's recommendations for liquid amounts, but avoid adding too much, as it can dilute the flavors.

●Avoid Lifting the Lid

One of the key principles of slow cooking is to maintain a consistent and slow cooking temperature. Avoid lifting the lid during the cooking process, as it can significantly extend the cooking time and compromise the final result.

●Adjust Seasonings to Taste

While slow cookers excel at infusing flavors, you may need to adjust seasonings at the end of the cooking process to suit your taste preferences. Taste the dish before serving and add additional seasoning if needed.

●Experiment and Adapt

Don't be afraid to experiment with the recipes or adapt them to your liking. Once you become comfortable with slow cooking, you can start creating your own variations and combinations.

Breakfast Recipes

Breakfast Recipes

Apple And Chia Mix

Servings: 2
Cooking Time: 8 Hours

Ingredients:
- ¼ cup chia seeds
- 2 apples, cored and roughly cubed
- 1 cup almond milk
- 2 tablespoons maple syrup
- 1 teaspoon vanilla extract
- ½ tablespoon cinnamon powder
- Cooking spray

Directions:
1. Grease your Crock Pot with the cooking spray, add the chia seeds, milk and the other ingredients, toss, put the lid on and cook on Low for 8 hours.
2. Divide the mix into bowls and serve for breakfast.

Nutrition Info:
- calories 453, fat 29.3, fiber 8, carbs 51.1, protein 3.4

Vegetable Omelet

Servings: 4
Cooking Time: 2 Hours 10 Minutes
Ingredients:
- 6 eggs
- ½ cup milk
- ¼ teaspoon salt
- Black pepper, to taste
- 1/8 teaspoon garlic powder
- 1/8 teaspoon chili powder
- 1 cup broccoli florets
- 1 red bell pepper, thinly sliced
- 1 small yellow onion, finely chopped
- 1 garlic clove, minced
- For Garnishing
- Chopped tomatoes
- Fresh parsley
- Shredded cheddar cheese
- Chopped onions

Directions:
1. Mix together eggs, milk, garlic powder, chili powder, salt and black pepper in a large mixing bowl.
2. Grease a crockpot and add garlic, onions, broccoli florets and sliced peppers.
3. Stir in the egg mixture and cover the lid.
4. Cook on HIGH for about 2 hours.
5. Top with cheese and allow it to stand for about 3 minutes.

6.Dish out the omelet into a serving plate and garnish with chopped onions, chopped tomatoes and fresh parsley.

Nutrition Info:
- Calories: 136 Fat: 7.4g Carbohydrates: 7.8g

Egg Bake

Servings: 8
Cooking Time: 8 Hours
Ingredients:

- 20 ounces tater tots
- 2 yellow onions, chopped
- 6 ounces bacon, chopped
- 2 cups cheddar cheese, shredded
- 12 eggs
- ¼ cup parmesan, grated
- 1 cup milk
- Salt and black pepper to the taste
- 4 tablespoons white flour
- Cooking spray

Directions:

1.Grease your Crock Pot with cooking spray and layer half of the tater tots, onions, bacon, cheddar and parmesan.
2.Continue layering the rest of the tater tots, bacon, onions, parmesan and cheddar.
3.In a bowl, mix the eggs with milk, salt, pepper and flour and whisk well.
4.Pour this into the Crock Pot, cover and cook on Low for 8 hours.
5.Slice, divide between plates and serve for breakfast.

Nutrition Info:
- calories 290, fat 9, fiber 1, carbs 9, protein 22

Peachy Cinnamon Butter

Servings: 8
Cooking Time: 8 Hrs
Ingredients:

- 15 oz. peach, pitted, peeled and cubed
- 2 cup of sugar
- ¼ tsp salt
- 1 tbsp ground cinnamon
- 1 tsp fresh ginger, peeled and grated
- 5 tbsp lemon juice

Directions:

1.Take a blender jug and add peach cubes into the jug.
2.Blender until peaches are pureed.
3.Pour this peach puree into the Crock Pot.
4.Stir in salt, sugar, grated ginger, and cinnamon.
5.Put the cooker's lid on and set the cooking time to 8 hours on Low settings.
6.Stir in lemon juice and mix well.
7.Add the peach butter to glass jars.
8.Allow the jars to cool and serve with bread.

Nutrition Info:
- Per Serving: Calories 141, Total Fat 0.1g, Fiber 1g, Total Carbs 37.03g, Protein 0g

Apricots Bread Pudding

Servings: 9
Cooking Time: 5 Hrs
Ingredients:

- 10 oz. French bread
- 6 tbsp dried apricots
- 10 oz. milk
- 3 eggs, beaten
- 4 tbsp butter
- ½ tsp salt
- 1 tsp vanilla sugar
- ½ tsp ground nutmeg
- ½ tsp ground cardamom
- ¼ cup whipped cream
- 4 tbsp brown sugar

Directions:

1. Melt butter by heating in a saucepan then add milk.
2. Cook until warm, then stir in vanilla sugar, salt, ground cardamom, ground nutmeg, and brown sugar.
3. Continue mixing the milk mixture until sugar is fully dissolved.
4. Spread French bread and dried apricots in the Crock Pot.
5. Beat eggs in a bowl and add to the milk mixture.
6. Stir in cream and mix well until fully incorporated.
7. Pour this milk-cream mixture over the bread and apricots in the Crock Pot.
8. Put the cooker's lid on and set the cooking time to 5 hours on Low settings.
9. Serve.

Nutrition Info:

- Per Serving: Calories 229, Total Fat 11.5g, Fiber 1g, Total Carbs 24.3g, Protein 8g

Egg Casserole

Servings: 4
Cooking Time: 6 Hours 30 Minutes
Ingredients:

- ¾ cup milk
- ½ teaspoon salt
- 8 large eggs
- ½ teaspoon dry mustard
- ¼ teaspoon black pepper
- 4 cups hash brown potatoes, partially thawed
- ½ cup green bell pepper, chopped
- 4 green onions, chopped
- 12 ounces ham, diced
- ½ cup red bell pepper, chopped
- 1½ cups cheddar cheese, shredded

Directions:

1. Whisk together eggs, dry mustard, milk, salt and black pepper in a large bowl.
2. Grease the crockpot and put 1/3 of the hash brown potatoes, salt and black pepper.
3. Layer with 1/3 of the diced ham, red bell peppers, green bell peppers, green onions and cheese.
4. Repeat the layers twice, ending with the cheese and top with the egg mixture.
5. Cover and cook on LOW for about 6 hours.
6. Serve this delicious casserole for breakfast.

Nutrition Info:

- Calories: 453 Fat: 26g Carbohydrates: 32.6g

Mix Vegetable Casserole

Servings: 8
Cooking Time: 4 Hrs
Ingredients:

- 4 egg whites
- 8 eggs
- Salt and black pepper to the taste
- 2 tsp ground mustard
- ¾ cup milk
- 30 oz. hash browns
- 4 bacon strips, cooked and chopped
- 1 broccoli head, chopped
- 2 bell peppers, chopped
- Cooking spray
- 6 oz. cheddar cheese, shredded
- 1 small onion, chopped

Directions:

1. Beat egg with black pepper, salt, milk, and mustard in a bowl.
2. Coat the base of your Crock Pot with cooking spray.
3. Place broccoli, onion, hash browns, and bell peppers in the cooker.
4. Pour the eggs on top and drizzle bacon and cheddar over it.
5. Put the cooker's lid on and set the cooking time to 4 hours on Low settings.
6. Serve.

Nutrition Info:

- Per Serving: Calories 300, Total Fat 4g, Fiber 8g, Total Carbs 18g, Protein 8g

Berry-berry Jam

Servings: 6
Cooking Time: 4 Hrs
Ingredients:

- 1 cup white sugar
- 1 cup strawberries
- 1 tbsp gelatin
- 3 tbsp water
- 1 tbsp lemon zest
- 1 tsp lemon juice
- ½ cup blueberries

Directions:

1. Take a blender jug and add berries, sugar, lemon juice, and lemon zest to puree.
2. Blend this blueberry-strawberry mixture for 3 minutes until smooth.
3. Pour this berry mixture into the base of your Crock Pot.
4. Put the cooker's lid on and set the cooking time to 1 hour on High settings.
5. Mix gelatin with 3 tbsp water in a bowl and pour it into the berry mixture.
6. Again, put the cooker's lid on and set the cooking time to 3 hours on High settings.
7. Allow the jam to cool down.
8. Serve.

Nutrition Info:

- Per Serving: Calories 163, Total Fat 8.3g, Fiber 2g, Total Carbs 20.48g, Protein 3g

Peppers, Kale And Cheese Omelet

Servings: 4
Cooking Time: 3 Hours
Ingredients:

- 1 teaspoon olive oil
- 7 ounces roasted red peppers, chopped
- 6 ounces baby kale
- Salt and black pepper to the taste
- 6 ounces feta cheese, crumbled
- ¼ cup green onions, sliced
- 7 eggs, whisked

Directions:

1.In a bowl, mix the eggs with cheese, kale, red peppers, green onions, salt and pepper, whisk well, pour into the Crock Pot after you've greased it with the oil, cover, cook on Low for 3 hours, divide between plates and serve right away.

Nutrition Info:

- calories 231, fat 7, fiber 4, carbs 7, protein 14

Feta Eggs

Servings:4
Cooking Time: 5 Hours
Ingredients:

- 4 eggs, beaten
- ¼ cup milk
- 4 oz Feta, crumbled
- 1 teaspoon olive oil
- 1 teaspoon dried thyme
- ¼ teaspoon salt

Directions:

1.Mix eggs with milk, salt, and thyme.
2.Then add olive oil and pour the mixture in the Crock Pot.
3.Top it with crumbled eggs and close the lid.
4.Cook the meal on Low for 5 hours.

Nutrition Info:

- Per Serving: 156 calories, 10.1g protein, 2.4g carbohydrates, 11.9g fat, 0.1g fiber, 190mg cholesterol, 533mg sodium, 87mg potassium

Sausage And Potato Mix

Servings: 2
Cooking Time: 6 Hours
Ingredients:

- 2 sweet potatoes, peeled and roughly cubed
- 1 green bell pepper, minced
- ½ yellow onion, chopped
- 4 ounces smoked andouille sausage, sliced
- 1 cup cheddar cheese, shredded
- ¼ cup Greek yogurt
- ¼ teaspoon basil, dried
- 1 cup chicken stock
- Salt and black pepper to the taste
- 1 tablespoon parsley, chopped

Directions:

1.In your Crock Pot, combine the potatoes with the bell pepper, sausage and the other ingredients, toss, put the lid on and cook on Low for 6 hours.

2.Divide between plates and serve for breakfast.

Nutrition Info:

- calories 623, fat 35.7, fiber 7.6, carbs 53.1, protein 24.8

Basil Sausages

Servings:5

Cooking Time: 4 Hours

Ingredients:

- 1-pound Italian sausages, chopped
- 1 teaspoon dried basil
- 1 tablespoon olive oil
- 1 teaspoon ground coriander
- ¼ cup of water

Directions:

1.Sprinkle the chopped sausages with ground coriander and dried basil and transfer in the Crock Pot.

2.Add olive oil and water.

3.Close the lid and cook the sausages on high for 4 hours.

Nutrition Info:

- Per Serving: 338 calories, 12.9g protein, 0.6g carbohydrates, 31.2g fat, 0g fiber, 69mg cholesterol, 664mg sodium, 231mg potassium.

Vanilla Maple Oats

Servings: 4

Cooking Time: 8 Hrs

Ingredients:

- 1 cup steel-cut oats
- 2 tsp vanilla extract
- 2 cups vanilla almond milk
- 2 tbsp maple syrup
- 2 tsp cinnamon powder
- 2 cups of water
- 2 tsp flaxseed
- Cooking spray
- 2 tbsp blackberries

Directions:

1.Coat the base of your Crock Pot with cooking spray.

2.Stir in oats, almond milk, vanilla extract, cinnamon, maple syrup, flaxseeds, and water.

3.Put the cooker's lid on and set the cooking time to 8 hours on Low settings.

4.Stir well and serve with blackberries on top.

5.Devour.

Nutrition Info:

- Per Serving: Calories 200, Total Fat 3g, Fiber 6g, Total Carbs 9g, Protein 3g

Greek Breakfast Casserole

Servings: 4
Cooking Time: 4 Hours
Ingredients:

- 2 eggs, whisked
- Salt and black pepper to the taste
- ½ cup milk
- 1 red onion, chopped
- 1 cup baby bell mushrooms, sliced
- ½ cup sun-dried tomatoes
- 1 teaspoon garlic, minced
- 2 cups spinach
- ½ cup feta cheese, crumbled

Directions:

1. In a bowl, mix the eggs with salt, pepper and milk and whisk well.
2. Add garlic, onion, mushrooms, spinach and tomatoes, toss well, pour this into your Crock Pot, sprinkle cheese all over, cover and cook on Low for 4 hours.
3. Slice, divide between plates and serve for breakfast.

Nutrition Info:

- calories 325, fat 7, fiber 7, carbs 27, protein 18

Thyme Hash Browns

Servings: 2
Cooking Time: 4 Hours
Ingredients:

Cooking spray
- 10 ounces hash browns
- 2 eggs, whisked
- ¼ cup heavy cream
- ¼ teaspoon garlic powder
- A pinch of salt and black pepper
- ½ cup mozzarella, shredded
- 1 tablespoon chives, chopped
- 1 tablespoon parsley, chopped

Directions:

1. Grease your Crock Pot with cooking spray, spread the hash browns on the bottom, add the eggs, cream and the other ingredients except the cheese and toss.
2. Sprinkle the cheese on top, put the lid on and cook on High for 4 hours.
3. Divide the mix between plates and serve for breakfast.

Nutrition Info:

- calories 516, fat 29.2, fiber 4.7, carbs 51.3, protein 12.3

Saucy Sriracha Red Beans

Servings: 5
Cooking Time: 6 Hrs
Ingredients:

- 1 cup red beans, soaked and drained
- 3 chicken stock
- 3 tbsp tomato paste
- 1 onion, sliced
- 1 tsp salt
- 1 chili pepper, sliced
- 1 tsp sriracha
- 1 tbsp butter
- 1 tsp turmeric
- 1 cup green peas

Directions:

1. Spread the red beans in the Crock Pot.
2. Add turmeric, salt, and chicken stock on its top.
3. Put the cooker's lid on and set the cooking time to 4 hours on High settings.
4. Toss the sliced onion with Sriracha, butter, chili pepper, and sriracha in a separate bowl.
5. Spread this onion-pepper mixture over the cooked beans in the Crock Pot.
6. Cover the beans again and slow cook for another 1 hour on Low setting.
7. Serve after a gentle stir.

Nutrition Info:

- Per Serving: Calories 190, Total Fat 3.1g, Fiber 8g, Total Carbs 31.6g, Protein 11g

Cheesy Quiche

Servings: 6
Cooking Time: 3 Hours
Ingredients:

- 1 pie crust
- 1 cup ham, cooked and chopped
- 2 cups Swiss cheese, shredded
- 6 eggs
- 1 cup whipping cream
- 4 green onions, chopped
- Salt and black pepper to the taste
- A pinch of nutmeg, ground
- Cooking spray

Directions:

1. Grease your Crock Pot with cooking spray, add pie crust inside, cover and cook on High for 1 hour and 30 minutes.
2. In a bowl, mix the eggs with salt, pepper, nutmeg and whipping cream and whisk well.
3. Pour this into pie crust, sprinkle cheese, ham and green onions, cover Crock Pot and cook on High for 1 hour and 30 minutes.
4. Slice quiche, divide it between plates and serve for breakfast.

Nutrition Info:

- calories 300, fat 4, fiber 7, carbs 15, protein 5

Appetizers Recipes

Appetizers Recipes

Quick Parmesan Bread

Servings: 8
Cooking Time: 1 1/4 Hours
Ingredients:

- 4 cups all-purpose flour
- 1/2 teaspoon salt
- 1/2 cup grated Parmesan cheese
- 1 teaspoon baking soda
- 2 cups buttermilk
- 2 tablespoons olive oil

Directions:

1. Mix the flour, salt, parmesan cheese and baking soda in a bowl.
2. Stir in the buttermilk and olive oil and mix well with a fork.
3. Shape the dough into a loaf and place it in your Crock Pot.
4. Cover with its lid and cook on high heat for 1 hour.
5. Serve the bread warm or chilled.

Chipotle Bbq Sausage Bites

Servings: 10
Cooking Time: 2 1/4 Hours
Ingredients:

- 3 pounds small smoked sausages
- 1 cup BBQ sauce
- 2 chipotle peppers in adobo sauce
- 1 tablespoon tomato paste
- 1/4 cup white wine
- Salt and pepper to taste

Directions:

1. Combine all the ingredients in your Crock Pot.
2. Add salt and pepper if needed and cover with a lid.
3. Cook on high settings for 2 hours.
4. Serve the sausage bites warm or chilled.

Cranberry Baked Brie

Servings: 6
Cooking Time: 2 1/4 Hours
Ingredients:

- 1 wheel of Brie
- 1/2 cup cranberry sauce
- 1/2 teaspoon dried thyme

Directions:

1. Spoon the cranberry sauce in your Crock Pot.
2. Sprinkle with thyme and top with the Brie cheese.
3. Cover with a lid and cook on low settings for 2 hours.
4. The cheese is best served warm with bread sticks or tortilla chips.

Marinara Turkey Meatballs

Servings: 8
Cooking Time: 6 1/2 Hours
Ingredients:

- 2 pounds ground turkey
- 1 carrot, grated
- 1 potato, grated
- 1 shallot, chopped
- 1 tablespoon chopped parsley
- 1 tablespoon chopped cilantro
- 4 basil leaves, chopped
- 1/2 teaspoon dried mint
- 1 egg
- 1/4 cup breadcrumbs
- Salt and pepper to taste
- 2 cups marinara sauce

Directions:

1. Mix the turkey, carrot, potato, shallot, parsley, cilantro, basil, mint, egg and breadcrumbs in a bowl.
2. Add salt and pepper to taste and mix well.
3. Pour the marinara sauce in your Crock Pot then form meatballs and drop them in the sauce.
4. Cover the pot with its lid and cook on low settings for 6 hours.
5. Serve the meatballs warm or chilled.

Mixed Olive Dip

Servings: 10
Cooking Time: 1 3/4 Hours
Ingredients:

- 1 pound ground chicken
- 2 tablespoons olive oil
- 1 green bell pepper, cored and diced
- 1/2 cup Kalamata olives, pitted and chopped
- 1/2 cup green olives, chopped
- 1/2 cup black olives, pitted and chopped
- 1 cup green salsa
- 1/2 cup chicken stock
- 1 cup grated Cheddar cheese
- 1/2 cup shredded mozzarella

Directions:

1. Combine all the ingredients in your Crock Pot.
2. Cover with its lid and cook on high settings for 1 1/2 hours.
3. The dip is best served warm.

Cheeseburger Meatballs

Servings 8
Cooking Time 6 14 Hours
Ingredients:

- 2 pounds ground pork
- 1 shallot, chopped
- 2 tablespoons beef stock
- 1 egg
- 14 cup breadcrumbs

- 1 teaspoon Cajun seasoning
- 12 teaspoon dried basil
- Salt and pepper to taste
- 2 cups shredded processed cheese

Directions:

1. Mix the pork, shallot, beef stock, egg, breadcrumbs, Cajun seasoning and basil in a bowl.
2. Add salt and pepper to taste and mix well.
3. Form small meatballs and place them in the Crock Pot.
4. Top with shredded cheese and cook on low settings for 6 hours.
5. Serve the meatballs warm.

Tahini Chickpea Dip

Servings: 6
Cooking Time: 6 1/4 Hours
Ingredients:

- 2 cups dried chickpeas, rinsed
- 5 cups water
- 1 bay leaf
- Salt and pepper to taste

- 1 lemon, juiced
- 1/4 cup tahini paste
- 2 tablespoons olive oil
- 1 pinch red pepper flakes

Directions:

1. Combine the chickpeas, water, bay leaf, salt and pepper in a Crock Pot.
2. Cook on low settings for 6 hours then drain and transfer in a food processor.
3. Stir in the remaining ingredients and pulse until smooth.
4. Spoon into a bowl and serve fresh or store in an airtight container in the fridge.

Hoisin Chicken Wings

Servings: 8
Cooking Time: 7 1/4 Hours
Ingredients:

- 4 pounds chicken wings
- 2/3 cup hoisin sauce
- 4 garlic cloves, minced
- 1 teaspoon grated ginger
- 1 teaspoon sesame oil

- 1 tablespoon molasses
- 1 teaspoon hot sauce
- 1/4 teaspoon ground black pepper
- 1/2 teaspoon salt

Directions:

1. Mix the hoisin sauce, garlic, ginger, sesame oil, molasses, hot sauce, black pepper and salt in your Crock

Pot.
2. Add the chicken wings and toss them around until evenly coated.
3. Cover with a lid and cook on low settings for 7 hours.
4. Serve the wings warm or chilled.

Chipotle Bbq Meatballs

Servings: 10
Cooking Time: 7 1/2 Hours
Ingredients:
- 3 pounds ground pork
- 2 garlic cloves, minced
- 2 shallots, chopped
- 2 chipotle peppers, chopped
- Salt and pepper to taste
- 2 cups BBQ sauce
- 1/4 cup cranberry sauce
- 1 bay leaf

Directions:
1. Mix the ground pork, garlic, shallots, chipotle peppers, salt and pepper in a bowl.
2. Combine the BBQ sauce, cranberry sauce, bay leaf, salt and pepper in your Crock Pot.
3. Form small meatballs and drop them in the sauce.
4. Cover the pot with its lid and cook on low settings for 7 hours.
5. Serve the meatballs warm or chilled with cocktail skewers or toothpicks.

Stuffed Artichokes

Servings: 6
Cooking Time: 6 1/2 Hours
Ingredients:
- 6 fresh artichokes
- 6 anchovy fillets, chopped
- 4 garlic cloves, minced
- 2 tablespoons olive oil
- 1 cup breadcrumbs
- 1 tablespoon chopped parsley
- Salt and pepper to taste
- 1/4 cup white wine

Directions:
1. Cut the stem of each artichoke so that it sits flat on your chopping board then cut the top off and trim the outer leaves, cleaning the center as well.
2. In a bowl, mix the anchovy fillets, garlic, olive oil, breadcrumbs and parsley. Add salt and pepper to taste.
3. Top each artichoke with breadcrumb mixture and rub it well into the leaves.
4. Place the artichokes in your Crock Pot and pour in the white wine.
5. Cook on low settings for 6 hours.
6. Serve the artichokes warm or chilled.

Chili Chicken Wings

Servings: 8
Cooking Time: 7 1/4 Hours
Ingredients:

- 4 pounds chicken wings
- 1/4 cup maple syrup
- 1 teaspoon garlic powder
- 1 teaspoon chili powder
- 2 tablespoons balsamic vinegar
- 1 tablespoon Dijon mustard
- 1 teaspoon Worcestershire sauce
- 1/2 cup tomato sauce
- 1 teaspoon salt

Directions:

1. Combine the chicken wings and the remaining ingredients in a Crock Pot.
2. Toss around until evenly coated and cook on low settings for 7 hours.
3. Serve the chicken wings warm or chilled.

Bacon Baked Potatoes

Servings: 8
Cooking Time: 3 1/4 Hours
Ingredients:

- 3 pounds new potatoes, halved
- 8 slices bacon, chopped
- 1 teaspoon dried rosemary
- 1/4 cup chicken stock
- Salt and pepper to taste

Directions:

1. Heat a skillet over medium flame and stir in the bacon. Cook until crisp.
2. Place the potatoes in a Crock Pot. Add the bacon bits and its fat, as well as rosemary, salt and pepper and mix until evenly distributed.
3. Pour in the stock and cook on high heat for 3 hours.
4. Serve the potatoes warm.

Blue Cheese Chicken Wings

Servings: 8
Cooking Time: 7 1/4 Hours
Ingredients:

- 4 pounds chicken wings
- 1/2 cup buffalo sauce
- 1/2 cup spicy tomato sauce
- 1 tablespoon tomato paste
- 2 tablespoons apple cider vinegar
- 1 tablespoon Worcestershire sauce
- 1 cup sour cream
- 2 oz. blue cheese, crumbled
- 1 thyme sprig

Directions:

1. Combine the buffalo sauce, tomato sauce, vinegar, Worcestershire sauce, sour cream, blue cheese and thyme in a Crock Pot.
2. Add the chicken wings and toss them until evenly coated.

3. Cook on low settings for 7 hours.
4. Serve the chicken wings preferably warm.

Pizza Dip

Servings: 20
Cooking Time: 6 1/4 Hours
Ingredients:

- 1 pound spicy sausages, sliced
- 1/2 pound salami, diced
- 1 red bell pepper, cored and diced
- 1 yellow bell pepper, cored and sliced
- 1 onion, chopped
- 2 garlic cloves, minced
- 2 cups tomato sauce
- 1/2 cup grated Parmesan
- 1 cup shredded mozzarella
- 1/2 teaspoon dried basil
- 1/2 teaspoon dried oregano

Directions:

1. Layer all the ingredients in your Crock Pot.
2. Cook on low settings for 6 hours, mixing once during the cooking time to ensure an even distribution of ingredients.
3. Serve the dip warm.

Bacon Wrapped Chicken Livers

Servings: 6
Cooking Time: 3 1/2 Hours
Ingredients:

- 2 pounds chicken livers
- Bacon slices as needed

Directions:

1. Wrap each chicken liver in one slice of bacon and place all the livers in your crock pot.
2. Cook on high heat for 3 hours.
3. Serve warm or chilled.

Spicy Chicken Taquitos

Servings: 8
Cooking Time: 6 1/2 Hours
Ingredients:

- 4 chicken breasts, cooked and diced
- 1 cup cream cheese
- 2 jalapeno peppers, chopped
- 1/2 cup canned sweet corn, drained
- 1/2 teaspoon cumin powder
- 4 garlic cloves, minced
- 16 taco-sized flour tortillas
- 2 cups grated Cheddar cheese

Directions:

1. In a bowl, mix the chicken, cream cheese, garlic, cumin, poblano peppers and corn. Stir in the cheese as well.

2. Place your tortillas on your working surface and top each tortilla with the cheese mixture.
3. Roll the tortillas tightly to form an even roll.
4. Place the rolls in your Crock Pot.
5. Cook on low settings for 6 hours.
6. Serve warm.

Beer Cheese Fondue

Servings: 8
Cooking Time: 2 1/4 Hours
Ingredients:

- 1 shallot, chopped
- 1 garlic clove, minced
- 1 cup grated Gruyere cheese
- 2 cups grated Cheddar
- 1 tablespoon cornstarch

- 1 teaspoon Dijon mustard
- 1/2 teaspoon cumin seeds
- 1 cup beer
- Salt and pepper to taste

Directions:

1. Combine the shallot, garlic, cheeses, cornstarch, mustard, cumin seeds and beer in your Crock Pot.
2. Add salt and pepper to taste and mix well.
3. Cover the pot with its lid and cook on high settings for 2 hours.
4. Serve the fondue warm.
5. Serve the fondue warm.

Beef, Pork & Lamb Recipes

Beef, Pork & Lamb Recipes

Beef Casserole

Servings:5
Cooking Time: 7 Hours
Ingredients:

- 7 oz ground beef
- 1 cup Cheddar cheese, shredded
- ½ cup cream
- 1 teaspoon Italian seasonings
- ½ cup broccoli, chopped

Directions:

1. Mix ground beef with Italian seasonings and put in the Crock Pot.
2. Top the meat with broccoli and Cheddar cheese.
3. Then pour the cream over the casserole mixture and close the lid.
4. Cook the casserole on Low for 7 hours.

Nutrition Info:

- Per Serving: 186 calories, 18.1g protein, 1.7g carbohydrates, 11.6g fat, 0.2g fiber, 64mg cholesterol, 178mg sodium, 220mg potassium.

Mussaman Curry

Servings:4
Cooking Time: 5 Hours
Ingredients:

- 16 oz beef sirloin, cubed
- 1 tablespoon curry powder
- 2 tablespoons coconut aminos
- 2 tablespoons soy sauce
- 1 tablespoon sesame oil
- 2 tablespoons peanut butter
- ¼ cup peanuts, chopped
- 1 cup coconut cream

Directions:

1. Mix curry powder with coconut aminos, soy sauce, sesame oil, and coconut cream.
2. After this, mix the curry mixture with beef and transfer in the Crock Pot.
3. Add all remaining ingredients and mix well.
4. Close the lid and cook the curry on High for 5 hours.

Nutrition Info:

- Per Serving: 494 calories, 40.8g protein, 9.4g carbohydrates, 33.5g fat, 3.2g fiber, 101mg cholesterol, 582mg sodium, 773mg potassium.

Ketchup Pork Ribs

Servings: 4
Cooking Time: 4 Hours
Ingredients:

- 1-pound pork ribs, roughly chopped
- 4 tablespoons ketchup
- 1 tablespoon fresh dill
- 1 tablespoon avocado oil
- ½ cup beef broth

Directions:

1. Mix pork ribs with ketchup and avocado oil.
2. Put them in the Crock Pot.
3. Add beef broth and dill.
4. Close the pork ribs on High for 4 hours.

Nutrition Info:

- Per Serving: 336 calories, 31.1g protein, 4.5g carbohydrates, 20.8g fat, 0.3g fiber, 117mg cholesterol, 330mg sodium, 447mg potassium

Jamaican Pork Mix

Servings: 4
Cooking Time: 4 Hours
Ingredients:

- 1 cup corn kernels, frozen
- 1 cup of water
- 1 teaspoon Jamaican spices
- 10 oz pork sirloin, chopped
- 1 tomato, chopped
- 1 teaspoon salt
- 1 teaspoon avocado oil

Directions:

1. Roast the chopped pork sirloin in the avocado oil for 1 minute per side.
2. Then mix the meat with Jamaican spices and transfer in the Crock Pot.
3. Add all remaining ingredients and close the lid.
4. Cook the meal on High for 4 hours.

Nutrition Info:

- Per Serving: 174 calories, 23.5g protein, 7.9g carbohydrates, 5.4g fat, 1.3g fiber, 65mg cholesterol, 629mg sodium, 412mg potassium

Barbacoa Beef

Servings: 4
Cooking Time: 5 Hours
Ingredients:

- 1-pound beef chuck roast
- 1 teaspoon ground black pepper
- ½ teaspoon salt
- 1 teaspoon ground cumin

- ¼ lime,
- ½ teaspoon ground clove

- 2 cups of water

Directions:
1. Put the beef in the Crock Pot.
2. Add ground black pepper, salt, ground cumin, ground clove, and water.
3. Close the lid and cook the meat on High for 5 hours.
4. Then shred the beef.
5. Squeeze the line over the meat and carefully mix.

Nutrition Info:
- Per Serving: 417 calories, 29.9g protein, 1.2g carbohydrates, 31.8g fat, 0.4g fiber, 117mg cholesterol, 369mg sodium, 283mg potassium.

Sweet Lamb Tagine

Servings:6
Cooking Time: 10 Hours
Ingredients:
- 12 oz lamb fillet, chopped
- 1 cup apricots, pitted, chopped
- 1 cup red wine
- 1 jalapeno pepper, sliced

- 1 teaspoon ground nutmeg
- 1 cup of water
- 1 teaspoon ground ginger

Directions:
1. Mix lamb with ground nutmeg and ground ginger.
2. Transfer the lamb meat in the Crock Pot.
3. Add water, jalapeno pepper, red wine, and apricots.
4. Close the lid and cook the tagine for 10 hours on Low.

Nutrition Info:
- Per Serving: 154 calories, 16.4g protein, 4.4g carbohydrates, 4.5g fat, 0.7g fiber, 51mg cholesterol, 47mg sodium, 307mg potassium.

Thai Cocoa Pork

Servings: 4
Cooking Time: 7 Hours
Ingredients:
- 2 tablespoons olive oil
- 2 pounds pork butt, boneless and cubed
- Salt and black pepper to the taste
- 6 eggs, hard-boiled, peeled and sliced
- 1 tablespoon cilantro, chopped
- 1 tablespoon coriander seeds
- 1 tablespoon ginger, grated

- 1 tablespoon black peppercorns
- 2 tablespoons garlic, chopped
- 2 tablespoons five spice powder
- 1 and ½ cup soy sauce
- 2 tablespoons cocoa powder
- 1 yellow onion, chopped
- 8 cups water

Directions:

1. In your Crock Pot, mix oil with pork, salt, pepper, cilantro, coriander, ginger, peppercorns, garlic, five spice, soy sauce, cocoa, onion and water, toss, cover and cook on Low for 7 hours.
2. Divide stew into bowls, add egg slices on top and serve.

Nutrition Info:

- calories 400, fat 10, fiber 9, carbs 28, protein 22

Naked Beef Enchilada In A Crockpot

Servings:4
Cooking Time: 6 Hours
Ingredients:

- 1-pound ground beef
- 2 tablespoons enchilada spice mix
- 1 cup cauliflower florets
- 2 cups Mexican cheese blend, grated
- ¼ cup cilantro, chopped

Directions:

1. In a skillet, sauté the ground beef over medium flame for 3 minutes.
2. Transfer to the crockpot and add the enchilada spice mix and cauliflower.
3. Stir to combine.
4. Add the Mexican cheese blend on top.
5. Cook on low for 6 hours or on high for 4 hours.
6. Sprinkle with cilantro on top.

Nutrition Info:

- Calories per serving: 481; Carbohydrates: 1g; Protein: 35.1g; Fat: 29.4g; Sugar: 0g; Sodium: 536mg; Fiber:0 g

Italian Sausage Soup

Servings: 12
Cooking Time: 6 Hours
Ingredients:

- 64 ounces chicken stock
- 1 teaspoon olive oil
- 1 cup heavy cream
- 10 ounces spinach
- 6 bacon slices, chopped
- 1 pound radishes, chopped
- 2 garlic cloves, minced
- Salt and black pepper to the taste
- A pinch of red pepper flakes, crushed
- 1 yellow onion, chopped
- 1 and ½ pounds hot pork sausage, chopped

Directions:

1. Heat up a pan with the oil over medium-high heat, add sausage, onion and garlic, stir, brown for a few minutes and transfer to your Crock Pot.

2. Add stock, spinach, radishes, bacon, cream, salt, pepper and red pepper flakes, stir, cover and cook on Low for 6 hours.
3. Ladle soup into bowls and serve.

Nutrition Info:
- calories 291, fat 22, fiber 2, carbs 14, protein 17

Beef Bolognese

Servings:4
Cooking Time: 5 Hours
Ingredients:
- ½ cup onion, diced
- 1 teaspoon dried basil
- 1 teaspoon dried cilantro
- ½ cup tomato juice
- 1 tablespoon sesame oil
- 1-pound ground beef
- 2 oz parmesan, grated

Directions:
1. In the mixing bowl mix ground beef with cilantro, basil, and onion.
2. Pour the sesame oil in the Crock Pot.
3. Add tomato juice and ground beef mixture.
4. Cook it on high for 3 hours.
5. Then add parmesan and carefully mix.
6. Cook the meal on low for 2 hours more.

Nutrition Info:
- Per Serving: 297 calories, 39.4g protein, 3.2g carbohydrates, 13.5g fat, 0.4g fiber, 111mg cholesterol, 289mg sodium, 548mg potassium.

Classic Pork Adobo

Servings:6
Cooking Time: 12 Hours
Ingredients:
- 2 pounds pork chops, sliced
- 4 cloves of garlic, minced
- 1 onion, chopped
- 2 bay leaves
- ¼ cup soy sauce
- ½ cup lemon juice, freshly squeezed
- 4 quail eggs, boiled and peeled

Directions:
1. Place all ingredients except the quail eggs in the CrockPot.
2. Give a good stir.
3. Close the lid and cook on high for 10 hours or on low for 12 hours.
4. Add in quail eggs an hour before the cooking time ends.

Nutrition Info:

- Calories per serving: 371; Carbohydrates: 6.4g; Protein: 40.7g; Fat: 24.1g; Sugar: 0g; Sodium: 720mg; Fiber: 3.9g

Sweet Pork Strips

Servings:2
Cooking Time: 5 Hours
Ingredients:

- 6 oz pork loin, cut into strips
- 1 tablespoon maple syrup
- 1 teaspoon ground paprika
- ½ teaspoon salt
- 1 teaspoon butter
- 1 cup of water

Directions:

1. Pour water in the Crock Pot.
2. Add salt and pork strips.
3. Cook the meat on High for 4 hours.
4. Then drain water and transfer the meat in the skillet.
5. Add butter, ground paprika, and roast the meat for 2 minutes per side.
6. Then sprinkle the meat with maple syrup and carefully mix.

Nutrition Info:

- Per Serving: 252 calories, 23.4g protein, 7.3g carbohydrates, 13.9g fat, 0.4g fiber, 73mg cholesterol, 652mg sodium, 407mg potassium

Aromatic Lamb

Servings:4
Cooking Time: Hours
Ingredients:

- 1 tablespoon minced garlic
- 1 teaspoon ground black pepper
- ½ teaspoon salt
- 1 teaspoon sesame oil
- 1-pound lamb sirloin, chopped
- ½ cup of water

Directions:

1. Mix the lamb with minced garlic, ground black pepper, and salt.
2. Then sprinkle the meat with sesame oil and transfer in the Crock Pot.
3. Add water and cook the meat on low for 8 hours.

Nutrition Info:

- Per Serving: 246 calories, 32.3g protein, 1g carbohydrates, 11.6g fat, 0.2g fiber, 104mg cholesterol, 373mg sodium, 393mg potassium.

Flank Steak With Arugula

Servings:4
Cooking Time: 10 Hours
Ingredients:

- 1-pound flank steak
- 1 teaspoon Worcestershire sauce
- Salt and pepper to taste
- 1 package arugula salad mix
- 2 tablespoon balsamic vinegar

Directions:

1. Season the flank steak with Worcestershire sauce, salt, and pepper.
2. Place in the crockpot that has been lined with aluminum foil.
3. Close the lid and cook on low for 10 hours or on high for 7 hours.
4. Meanwhile, prepare the salad by combining the arugula salad mix and balsamic vinegar. Set aside in the fridge.
5. Once the steak is cooked, allow to cool before slicing.
6. Serve on top of the arugula salad.

Nutrition Info:

- Calories per serving: 452; Carbohydrates: 5.8g; Protein: 30.2g; Fat:29.5g; Sugar: 1.2g; Sodium: 563mg; Fiber:3 g

Delightful Pepperoncini Beef

Servings:4
Cooking Time: 5 Hours
Ingredients:

- 2 oz pepperoncini
- 1-pound beef chuck roast
- 2 cups of water
- 1 teaspoon minced garlic

Directions:

1. Chop the beef roughly and mix with minced garlic.
2. Then transfer the beef in the Crock Pot.
3. Add water and pepperoncini.
4. Close the lid and cook the meal on High for 5 hours.

Nutrition Info:

- Per Serving: 418 calories, 29.9g protein, 1.7g carbohydrates, 31.6g fat, 0g fiber, 117mg cholesterol, 216mg sodium, 263mg potassium.

Jamaican Pork Shoulder

Servings: 12
Cooking Time: 7 Hrs.
Ingredients:

- ½ cup beef stock
- 1 tbsp olive oil
- ¼ cup keto Jamaican spice mix
- 4 lbs. pork shoulder

Directions:

1. Add pork, Jamaican spice mix and all other ingredients to the Crock Pot.
2. Put the cooker's lid on and set the cooking time to 7 hours on Low settings.
3. Slice the roast and serve warm.

Nutrition Info:

- Per Serving: Calories: 400, Total Fat: 6g, Fiber: 7g, Total Carbs: 10g, Protein: 25g

Ham Terrine

Servings:4
Cooking Time: 8 Hours
Ingredients:

- 2 smoked ham hock, cooked
- 1 onion, chopped
- 1 carrot, grated
- 1 tablespoon fresh parsley, chopped
- 1 tablespoon mustard
- 3 oz prosciutto, sliced
- 1 teaspoon sunflower oil
- 1 cup of water

Directions:

1. Chop the ham hock into small pieces and mix with onion, carrot, parsley, and mustard.
2. Then brush the loaf mold with sunflower oil from inside.
3. Make the pie crust from prosciutto in the loaf mold.
4. Add ham hock mixture over the prosciutto and wrap it.
5. Pour water in the Crock Pot.
6. Then insert the loaf mild with terrine inside and close the lid.
7. Cook the meal on Low for 8 hours.

Nutrition Info:

- Per Serving: 179 calories, 17.9g protein, 5.4g carbohydrates, 9.3g fat, 1.4g fiber, 52mg cholesterol, 296mg sodium, 334mg potassium

Fish & Seafood Recipes

Fish & Seafood Recipes

Chives Shrimp

Servings: 2
Cooking Time: 1 Hour
Ingredients:

- 1 pound shrimp, peeled and deveined
- 1 tablespoon chives, chopped
- ½ teaspoon basil, dried
- 1 teaspoon turmeric powder
- 1 tablespoon olive oil
- ½ cup chicken stock

Directions:

1. In your Crock Pot, mix the shrimp with the basil, chives and the other ingredients, toss, put the lid on and cook on High for 1 hour.
2. Divide the shrimp between plates and serve with a side salad.

Nutrition Info:

- calories 200, fat 12, fiber 3, carbs 7, protein 9

Cod Bacon Chowder

Servings: 6
Cooking Time: 3 Hrs
Ingredients:

- 1 yellow onion, chopped
- 10 oz. cod, cubed
- 3 oz. bacon, sliced
- 1 tsp sage
- 5 oz. potatoes, peeled and cubed
- 1 carrot, grated
- 5 cups of water
- 1 tbsp almond milk
- 1 tsp ground coriander
- 1 tsp salt

Directions:

1. Place grated carrots and onion in the Crock Pot.
2. Add almond milk, coriander, water, sage, fish, potatoes, and bacon.
3. Put the cooker's lid on and set the cooking time to 3 hours on High settings.
4. Garnish with chopped parsley.
5. Serve.

Nutrition Info:

- Per Serving: Calories 108, Total Fat 4.5g, Fiber 2g, Total Carbs 8.02g, Protein 10g

Lemon Trout

Servings:4
Cooking Time: 5 Hours
Ingredients:

- 1-pound trout, peeled, cleaned
- 1 lemon, sliced
- 1 teaspoon dried thyme
- 1 teaspoon ground black pepper
- 1 tablespoon olive oil
- ½ teaspoon salt
- ½ cup of water

Directions:

1. Rub the fish with dried thyme, ground black pepper, and salt.
2. Then fill the fish with sliced lemon and sprinkle with olive oil.
3. Place the trout in the Crock Pot and add water.
4. Cook the fish on Low for 5 hours.

Nutrition Info:

- Per Serving: 252 calories, 30.4g protein, 1.9g carbohydrates, 13.2g fat, 0.6g fiber, 84mg cholesterol, 368mg sodium, 554mg potassium.

Crockpot Fish Chowder

Servings:9
Cooking Time: 3 Hours
Ingredients:

- 2 pounds catfish fillet, sliced
- 2 tablespoons butter
- ½ cup fresh oysters
- 1 onion, chopped
- 2 cups water
- 1 red bell pepper, chopped
- 1 yellow bell pepper, chopped
- Salt and pepper to taste
- 1 cup full-fat milk

Directions:

1. Place all ingredients in the CrockPot.
2. Give a good stir.
3. Close the lid and cook on high for 2 hours or on low for 3 hours.

Nutrition Info:

- Calories per serving: 172; Carbohydrates:6.1 g; Protein: 20.5g; Fat: 9.4g; Sugar: 1.3g; Sodium: 592mg; Fiber: 3.5g

Orange Salmon

Servings: 2
Cooking Time: 2 Hours
Ingredients:

- 2 lemons, sliced
- 1 pound wild salmon, skinless and cubed
- ¼ cup balsamic vinegar
- ¼ cup red orange juice
- 1 teaspoon olive oil
- 1/3 cup orange marmalade

Directions:

1. Heat up a Crock Pot over medium heat, add vinegar, orange juice and marmalade, stir well, bring to a simmer for 1 minute and transfer to your Crock Pot.
2. Add salmon, lemon slices and oil, toss, cover and cook on High for 2 hours.
3. Divide salmon plates and serve with a side salad.

Nutrition Info:

- calories 260, fat 3, fiber 2, carbs 16, protein 8

Ginger Cod

Servings:6
Cooking Time: 5 Hours
Ingredients:

- 6 cod fillets
- 1 teaspoon minced ginger
- 1 tablespoon olive oil
- ¼ teaspoon minced garlic
- ¼ cup chicken stock

Directions:

1. In the mixing bowl mix minced ginger with olive oil and minced garlic.
2. Gently rub the fish fillets with the ginger mixture and put in the Crock Pot.
3. Add chicken stock.
4. Cook the cod on Low for 5 hours.

Nutrition Info:

- Per Serving: 112 calories, 20.1g protein, 0.3g carbohydrates, 3.4g fat, 0g fiber, 55mg cholesterol, 102mg sodium, 5mg potassium

Crispy Mackerel

Servings: 4
Cooking Time: 2 Hrs.
Ingredients:

- 4 mackerels
- 3 oz. breadcrumbs
- Juice and rind of 1 lemon
- 1 tbsp chives, finely chopped
- Salt and black pepper to the taste
- 1 egg, whisked
- 1 tbsp butter
- 1 tbsp vegetable oil
- 3 lemon wedges

Directions:
1. Whisk breadcrumbs with lemon rinds, lemon juice, chives, egg, black pepper, and salt in a small bowl.
2. Coat the mackerel with this breadcrumb's mixture liberally.
3. Brush the insert of your Crock Pot with butter and oil.
4. Place the mackerel along with breadcrumbs mixture to the cooker.
5. Put the cooker's lid on and set the cooking time to 2 hours on High settings.
6. Garnish with lemon wedges.
7. Enjoy.

Nutrition Info:
- Per Serving: Calories: 200, Total Fat: 3g, Fiber: 1g, Total Carbs: 3g, Protein: 12g

Thai Salmon Cakes

Servings: 10
Cooking Time: 6 Hrs.
Ingredients:

- 6 oz squid, minced
- 10 oz salmon fillet, minced
- 2 tbsp chili paste
- 1 tsp cayenne pepper
- 2 oz lemon leaves
- 3 tbsp green peas, mashed
- 2 tsp fish sauce
- 2 egg white

- 1 egg yolk
- 1 tsp oyster sauce
- 1 tsp salt
- ½ tsp ground coriander
- 1 tsp sugar
- 2 tbsp butter
- ¼ cup cream
- 3 tbsp almond flour

Directions:
1. Mix seafood with chili paste, cayenne pepper, lemon leaves, mashed green peas, fish sauce, whisked egg yolk and egg whites in a bowl.
2. Stir in sugar, salt, oyster sauce, sugar, almond flour, and ground coriander.
3. Mix well, then make small-sized fish cakes out of this mixture.
4. Add cream and butter to the insert of the Crock Pot.
5. Place the fish cakes in the butter and cream.
6. Put the cooker's lid on and set the cooking time to 5 hours on Low settings.
7. Serve warm with cream mixture.

Nutrition Info:
- Per Serving: Calories: 112, Total Fat: 6.7g, Fiber: 1g, Total Carbs: 2.95g, Protein: 10g

Rice Stuffed Squid

Servings: 4
Cooking Time: 3 Hrs.
Ingredients:

- 3 squids
- Tentacles from 1 squid, chopped
- 1 cup sticky rice
- 14 oz. dashi stock
- 2 tbsp sake
- 4 tbsp soy sauce
- 1 tbsp mirin
- 2 tbsp sugar

Directions:

1. Toss the chopped tentacles with rice and stuff the 3 squids with rice mixture.
2. Seal the squid using toothpicks then place them in the Crock Pot.
3. Add soy sauce, stock, sugar, sake, and mirin to the squids.
4. Put the cooker's lid on and set the cooking time to 3 hours on High settings.
5. Serve warm.

Nutrition Info:

- Per Serving: Calories: 230, Total Fat: 4g, Fiber: 4g, Total Carbs: 7g, Protein: 11g

Baked Cod

Servings:2
Cooking Time: 5 Hours
Ingredients:

- 2 cod fillets
- 2 teaspoons cream cheese
- 2 tablespoons bread crumbs
- 1 teaspoon salt
- ½ teaspoon cayenne pepper
- 2 oz Mozzarella, shredded

Directions:

1. Sprinkle the cod fillets with cayenne pepper and salt.
2. Put the fish in the Crock Pot.
3. Then top it with cream cheese, bread crumbs, and Mozzarella.
4. Close the lid and cook the meal for 5 hours on Low.

Nutrition Info:

- Per Serving: 210 calories, 29.2g protein, 6.2g carbohydrates, 7.6g fat, 0.4g fiber, 74mg cholesterol, 1462mg sodium, 26mg potassium

Spicy Cajun Scallops

Servings:6
Cooking Time: 2 Hours
Ingredients:

- 2 pounds scallops
- 2 teaspoon Cajun seasoning
- 2 tablespoons unsalted butter
- 1 teaspoon cayenne pepper
- Salt and pepper to taste

Directions:
1. Place everything in the crockpot.
2. Give a stir to combine all ingredients.
3. Close the lid and cook on low for 2 hours or on high for 45 minutes.

Nutrition Info:
- Calories per serving: 135; Carbohydrates: 2g; Protein: 19.5g; Fat: 7.2g; Sugar: 0g; Sodium: 384mg; Fiber: 1.4g

Mustard-crusted Salmon

Servings:4
Cooking Time: 4 Hours
Ingredients:
- 4 pieces salmon fillets
- salt and pepper to taste
- 2 teaspoons lemon juice
- 2 tablespoons stone-ground mustard
- ¼ cup full sour cream

Directions:
1. Season salmon fillets with salt and pepper to taste. Sprinkle with lemon juice.
2. Rub the stone-ground mustard all over the fillets.
3. Place inside the crockpot and cook on high for 2 hours or on low for 4 hours.
4. An hour before the cooking time, pour in the sour cream on top of the fish.
5. Continue cooking until the fish becomes flaky.

Nutrition Info:
- Calories per serving: 74; Carbohydrates: 4.2g; Protein: 25.9g; Fat:13.8 g; Sugar: 1.3g; Sodium: 536mg; Fiber: 2.5g

Crockpot Seafood Jambalaya

Servings:7
Cooking Time: 3 Hours
Ingredients:
- 1 onion, chopped
- 2 tablespoons olive oil
- 2 ribs of celery, sliced
- 1 green bell pepper, seeded and chopped
- 1 cup tomatoes, crushed
- 1 cup chicken broth
- 2 teaspoons dried oregano
- 2 teaspoons dried parsley
- 2 teaspoons organic Cajun seasoning
- 1 teaspoon cayenne pepper
- 1-pound shrimps, shelled and deveined
- ½ pound squid, cleaned
- 2 cups grated cauliflower

Directions:
1. Place all ingredients in the CrockPot.
2. Give a good stir.

3. Close the lid and cook on high for 2 hours or on low for 3 hours.

Nutrition Info:
- Calories per serving: 205; Carbohydrates: 5.9g; Protein: 26.7g; Fat: 10.5g; Sugar: 0.2g; Sodium: 830mg; Fiber: 3.2g

Chinese Miso Mackerel

Servings: 4
Cooking Time: 2 Hrs.
Ingredients:
- 2 lbs. mackerel, cut into medium pieces
- 1 cup of water
- 1 garlic clove, crushed
- 1 shallot, sliced
- 1-inch ginger piece, chopped
- 1/3 cup sake
- 1/3 cup mirin
- ¼ cup miso
- 1 sweet onion, thinly sliced
- 2 celery stalks, sliced
- 1 tbsp rice vinegar
- 1 tsp Japanese hot mustard
- Salt to the taste
- 1 tsp sugar

Directions:
1. Add mirin, sake, shallot, garlic, ginger, water, miso, and mackerel to the insert of the Crock Pot.
2. Put the cooker's lid on and set the cooking time to 2 hours on High settings.
3. Soak onion and celery in a bowl filled with ice water.
4. Drain the celery and onion, then toss them with sugar, salt, and mustard.
5. Serve the cooked mackerel with the onion-celery mixture.
6. Enjoy warm.

Nutrition Info:
- Per Serving: Calories: 300, Total Fat: 12g, Fiber: 1g, Total Carbs: 14g, Protein: 20g

Tuna With Chimichurri Sauce

Servings: 4
Cooking Time: 1 Hr. 15 Minutes
Ingredients:
- ½ cup cilantro, chopped
- 1/3 cup olive oil
- 1 small red onion, chopped
- 3 tbsp balsamic vinegar
- 2 tbsp parsley, chopped
- 2 tbsp basil, chopped
- 1 jalapeno pepper, chopped
- 1 lb. tuna steak, boneless, skinless and cubed
- Salt and black pepper to the taste
- 1 tsp red pepper flakes
- 2 garlic cloves, minced
- 1 tsp thyme, chopped
- A pinch of cayenne pepper
- 2 avocados, pitted, peeled and sliced
- 6 oz. baby arugula

Directions:
1. Whisk jalapeno, oil, vinegar, cilantro, onion, garlic, basil, pepper flakes, parsley, thyme, black pepper, salt,

and thyme in the Crock Pot.
2. Put the cooker's lid on and set the cooking time to 1 hour on High settings.
3. Now add tuna and cover again to cook for 15 minutes on High settings.
4. Slice the cooked tuna and serve warm with its sauce, arugula, and avocado slices.
5. Enjoy.

Nutrition Info:
- Per Serving: Calories: 186, Total Fat: 3g, Fiber: 1g, Total Carbs: 4g, Protein: 20g

Clams In Coconut Sauce

Servings:2
Cooking Time: 2 Hours
Ingredients:
- 1 cup coconut cream
- 1 teaspoon minced garlic
- 1 teaspoon chili flakes
- 1 teaspoon salt
- 1 teaspoon ground coriander
- 8 oz clams

Directions:
1. Pour coconut cream in the Crock Pot.
2. Add minced garlic, chili flakes, salt, and ground coriander.
3. Cook the mixture on high for 1 hour.
4. Then add clams and stir the meal well. Cook it for 1 hour on high more.

Nutrition Info:
- Per Serving: 333 calories, 3.5g protein, 19.6g carbohydrates, 28.9g fat, 3.1g fiber, 0mg cholesterol, 1592mg sodium, 425mg potassium.

Sweet Salmon

Servings:4
Cooking Time: 1.5 Hours
Ingredients:
- 1-pound salmon fillet
- 1 teaspoon Italian seasonings
- 1 tablespoon butter
- 1 tablespoon maple syrup
- ½ teaspoon salt
- 1 cup of water

Directions:
1. Pour water in the Crock Pot.
2. Add salt, salmon, and Italian seasonings.
3. Cook the fish on high for 1.5 hours.
4. Then melt the butter in the skillet and add maple syrup. Stir the mixture until smooth.
5. Add the cooked salmon and roast it on high heat for 2 minutes per side.

Nutrition Info:
- Per Serving: 192 calories, 22g protein, 3.5g carbohydrates, 10.2g fat, 0g fiber, 58mg cholesterol, 364mg sodium, 448mg potassium.

Poultry Recipes

Poultry Recipes

Pesto Chicken Mix

Servings: 2
Cooking Time: 6 Hours And 10 Minutes
Ingredients:

- 1 pound chicken breast, skinless, boneless and cut into strips
- 1 tablespoon basil pesto
- 1 tablespoon olive oil
- 4 scallions, chopped
- ½ cup kalamata olives, pitted and halved
- 1 cup chicken stock
- 1 tablespoon cilantro, chopped
- A pinch of salt and black pepper

Directions:

1. Heat up a pan with the oil over medium-high heat, add the scallions and the meat, brown for 10 minutes, transfer to the Crock Pot and mix with the remaining ingredients.
2. Toss, put the lid on, cook on Low for 6 hours, divide the mix between plates and serve.

Nutrition Info:

- calories 263, fat 14, fiber 1, carbs 8, protein 12

Chicken And Broccoli

Servings: 2
Cooking Time: 5 Hours
Ingredients:

- 1 pound chicken breast, skinless, boneless and sliced
- 1 cup broccoli florets
- ½ cup tomato sauce
- ½ cup chicken stock
- 1 tablespoon avocado oil
- 1 yellow onion, sliced
- 3 garlic cloves, minced
- A pinch of salt and black pepper
- 1 tablespoon cilantro, chopped

Directions:

1. In your Crock Pot, mix the chicken with the broccoli, tomato sauce and the other ingredients, toss, put the lid on and cook on High for 5 hours.
2. Divide the mix between plates and serve hot.

Nutrition Info:

- calories 253, fat 14, fiber 2, carbs 7, protein 16

Turkey With Rice

Servings: 2
Cooking Time: 7 Hours
Ingredients:

- 1 pound turkey breasts, skinless, boneless and cubed
- 1 cup wild rice
- 2 cups chicken stock
- 1 tablespoon cilantro, chopped
- 1 tablespoon oregano, chopped
- 2 tablespoons green onions, chopped
- ½ teaspoon coriander, ground
- ½ teaspoon rosemary, dried
- ½ teaspoon turmeric powder
- A pinch of salt and black pepper

Directions:

1. In your Crock Pot, mix the turkey with the rice, stock and the other ingredients, toss, put the lid on and cook on Low for 7 hours.
2. Divide everything between plates and serve.

Nutrition Info:

- calories 232, fat 12, fiber 2, carbs 6, protein 15

Romano Chicken Thighs

Servings: 4
Cooking Time: 4 Hrs
Ingredients:

- 6 chicken things, boneless and skinless and cut into medium chunks
- Salt and black pepper to the taste
- ½ cup white flour
- 2 tbsp olive oil
- 10 oz. tomato sauce
- 1 tsp white wine vinegar
- 4 oz. mushrooms, sliced
- 1 tbsp sugar
- 1 tbsp oregano, dried
- 1 tsp garlic, minced
- 1 tsp basil, dried
- 1 yellow onion, chopped
- 1 cup Romano cheese, grated

Directions:

1. Grease the base of the Crock Pot with oil.
2. Stir in chicken pieces and all other ingredients to the Crock Pot.
3. Put the cooker's lid on and set the cooking time to 4 hours on High settings.
4. Serve warm.

Nutrition Info:

- Per Serving: Calories: 430, Total Fat: 12g, Fiber: 6g, Total   Carbs: 25g, Protein: 60g

Pepperoni Chicken

Servings: 6
Cooking Time: 6 Hours
Ingredients:

- 14 ounces pizza sauce
- 1 tablespoon olive oil
- 4 medium chicken breasts, skinless and boneless
- Salt and black pepper to the taste

- 1 teaspoon oregano, dried
- 6 ounces mozzarella, sliced
- 1 teaspoon garlic powder
- 2 ounces pepperoni, sliced

Directions:

1. Put the chicken in your Crock Pot, add pizza sauce, oil, salt, pepper, garlic powder, pepperoni and mozzarella, cover and cook on Low for 6 hours.
2. Toss everything, divide between plates and serve.

Nutrition Info:

- calories 320, fat 10, fiber 6, carbs 14, protein 27

Cumin Chicken Mix

Servings: 2
Cooking Time: 6 Hours
Ingredients:

- 1 pound chicken breast, skinless, boneless and cubed
- 2 teaspoons olive oil
- ½ cup tomato sauce
- ¼ cup chicken stock
- ½ teaspoon garam masala
- ½ teaspoon chili powder

- ½ teaspoon cumin, ground
- 1 yellow onion, chopped
- ½ teaspoon sweet paprika
- A pinch of salt and black pepper
- 1 tablespoon chives, chopped

Directions:

1. In your Crock Pot, mix the chicken with the oil, tomato sauce, stock and the other ingredients, toss, put the lid on and cook on Low for 6 hours.
2. Divide everything between plates and serve right away.

Nutrition Info:

- calories 252, fat 12, fiber 4, carbs 7, protein 13

Sweet Potato Jalapeno Stew

Servings: 8
Cooking Time: 8 Hrs
Ingredients:

- 1 yellow onion, chopped
- ½ cup red beans, dried
- 2 red bell peppers, chopped
- 2 tbsp ginger, grated

- 4 garlic cloves, minced
- 2 lbs. sweet, peeled and cubed
- 3 cups chicken stock
- 14 oz. canned tomatoes, chopped

- 2 jalapeno peppers, chopped
- Salt and black pepper to the taste
- ½ tsp cumin, ground
- ½ tsp coriander, ground
- ¼ tsp cinnamon powder
- To Garnish:
- ¼ cup peanuts, roasted and chopped
- Juice of ½ lime

Directions:
1. Add red beans along with all other ingredients to the Crock Pot.
2. Put the cooker's lid on and set the cooking time to 8 hours on Low settings.
3. Garnish with peanuts and lime juice.
4. Serve warm.

Nutrition Info:
- Per Serving: Calories 259, Total Fat 8g, Fiber 7g, Total Carbs 42g, Protein 8g

Creamy Bacon Chicken

Servings: 4
Cooking Time: 12 Hours
Ingredients:

- 5 oz. bacon, cooked
- 8 oz. chicken breast
- 1 garlic clove, peeled and chopped
- ½ carrot, peeled and chopped
- 1 cup heavy cream
- 1 egg, beaten
- 1 tbsp paprika
- 1 tsp curry
- 3 tbsp chives, chopped
- 3 oz. scallions, chopped

Directions:
1. Carve a cut in the chicken breasts from sideways.
2. Stuff the chicken with garlic clove and carrot.
3. Place the stuffed chicken in the Crock Pot.
4. Mix egg with cream, paprika, curry, scallions, and paprika in a bowl.
5. Pour this curry mixture over the chicken and top it with chives and bacon.
6. Add the remaining ingredients to the cooker.
7. Put the cooker's lid on and set the cooking time to 12 hours on Low settings.
8. Shred the slow-cooked chicken and return to the cooker.
9. Mix well and serve.

Nutrition Info:
- Per Serving: Calories: 362, Total Fat: 29.6g, Fiber: 3g, Total Carbs: 7.17g, Protein: 19g

Stuffed Chicken Breast

Servings:4
Cooking Time: 6 Hours
Ingredients:

- 1-pound chicken breast, skinless, boneless
- 1 tomato, sliced
- 2 oz mozzarella, sliced
- 1 teaspoon fresh basil
- 1 teaspoon olive oil
- 1 teaspoon salt
- 1 cup of water

Directions:

1. Make the horizontal cut in the chicken breast in the shape of the pocket.
2. Then fill it with sliced mozzarella, tomato, and basil.
3. Secure the cut with the help of the toothpicks and sprinkle the chicken with olive oil and salt.
4. Place it in the Crock Pot and add water.
5. Cook the chicken on low for 6 hours.

Nutrition Info:

- Per Serving: 182 calories, 28.2g protein, 1.1g carbohydrates, 6.5g fat, 0.2g fiber, 80mg cholesterol, 727mg sodium, 458mg potassium.

Turkey Curry

Servings: 4
Cooking Time: 4 Hours
Ingredients:

- 18 ounces turkey meat, minced
- 3 ounces spinach
- 20 ounces canned tomatoes, chopped
- 2 tablespoons coconut oil
- 2 tablespoons coconut cream
- 2 garlic cloves, minced
- 2 yellow onions, sliced
- 1 tablespoon coriander, ground
- 2 tablespoons ginger, grated
- 1 tablespoons turmeric powder
- 1 tablespoon cumin, ground
- Salt and black pepper to the taste
- 2 tablespoons chili powder

Directions:

1. In your Crock Pot, mix turkey with spinach, tomatoes, oil, cream, garlic, onion, coriander, ginger, turmeric, cumin, chili, salt and pepper, stir, cover and cook on High for 4 hours.
2. Divide into bowls and serve.

Nutrition Info:

- calories 240, fat 4, fiber 3, carbs 13, protein 12

Sesame Chicken Wings

Servings: 4
Cooking Time: 4 Hrs
Ingredients:

- 1 lb. chicken wings
- ½ cup fresh parsley, chopped
- 1 tsp salt
- 1 tsp ground black pepper
- ¼ cup milk
- 1 tbsp sugar
- 5 tbsp honey
- 2 tbsp sesame seeds
- ¼ cup chicken stock
- 1 tsp soy sauce

Directions:

1. Rub the chicken wings with salt and black pepper.
2. Add this chicken to the Crock Pot along with chicken stock and parsley.
3. Put the cooker's lid on and set the cooking time to 4 hours on High settings.
4. Mix milk with honey, sugar, and sesame seeds in a bowl.
5. Transfer the chicken to a baking tray.
6. Pour the sesame mixture over the chicken wings.
7. Bake them for 10 minutes at 350 degrees F in a preheated oven.
8. Enjoy.

Nutrition Info:

- Per Serving: Calories: 282, Total Fat: 7.5g, Fiber: 1g, Total Carbs: 27.22g, Protein: 27g

Pomegranate Turkey

Servings: 4
Cooking Time: 4.5 Hours
Ingredients:

- 1 lb. turkey fillet, diced
- ½ cup pomegranate juice
- 2 oz. pomegranate juice
- 1 tbsp soy sauce
- 1 tbsp potato starch
- 1 tsp garlic powder
- ¼ cup onion, grated
- 1 tsp butter, melted
- 3 tbsp brown sugar
- 1 tsp salt
- 1 tsp ground white pepper

Directions:

1. Mix turkey with garlic powder, salt, onion, white pepper in a bowl and leave it for 10 minutes.
2. Transfer the turkey to the Crock Pot along with butter and pomegranate juice.
3. Put the cooker's lid on and set the cooking time to 3 hours on High settings.
4. Mix potato starch with soy sauce, 2 oz. pomegranate juice in a bowl.
5. Pour this mixture into the Crock Pot.
6. Put the cooker's lid on and set the cooking time to 1.5 hours on High settings.
7. Serve warm.

Nutrition Info:

- Per Serving: Calories: 676, Total Fat: 52.5g, Fiber: 3g, Total Carbs: 26.15g, Protein: 24g

Lemon Chicken Thighs

Servings:4
Cooking Time: 7 Hours
Ingredients:

- 4 chicken thighs, skinless, boneless
- 1 lemon, sliced
- 1 teaspoon ground black pepper
- ½ teaspoon ground nutmeg
- 1 teaspoon olive oil
- 1 cup of water

Directions:

1. Rub the chicken thighs with ground black pepper, nutmeg, and olive oil.
2. Then transfer the chicken in the Crock Pot.
3. Add lemon and water.
4. Close the lid and cook the meal on LOW for 7 hours.

Nutrition Info:

- Per Serving: 294 calories, 42.5g protein, 1.8g carbohydrates, 12.2g fat, 0.6g fiber, 130mg cholesterol, 128mg sodium, 383mg potassium.

Chicken And Sauce(1)

Servings: 8
Cooking Time: 4 Hours
Ingredients:

- 1 whole chicken, cut into medium pieces
- 1 tablespoon olive oil
- 1 and ½ tablespoons lemon juice
- 1 cup chicken stock
- 1 tablespoon cilantro, chopped
- 1 teaspoon cinnamon powder
- Salt and black pepper to the taste
- 1 tablespoon sweet paprika
- 1 teaspoon onion powder

Directions:

1. In your Crock Pot, mix chicken with oil, lemon juice, stock, cilantro, cinnamon, salt, pepper, paprika and onion powder, stir, cover and cook on High for 4 hours.
2. Divide chicken between plates and serve with cooking sauce drizzled on top.

Nutrition Info:

- calories 261, fat 4, fiber 6, carbs 12, protein 22

Green Chicken Salad

Servings:4
Cooking Time: 3.5 Hours
Ingredients:

- 1 cup celery stalk, chopped
- 10 oz chicken fillet
- 1 teaspoon salt
- 1 teaspoon ground black pepper
- 1 cup of water
- 1 tablespoon mustard
- 1 tablespoon mayonnaise
- 1 teaspoon lemon juice
- 1 cup arugula, chopped
- 1 cup of green grapes

Directions:
1. Put the chicken in the Crock Pot.
2. Add salt and ground black pepper. Add water.
3. Cook the chicken in high for 5 hours.
4. Meanwhile, put green grapes, arugula, and celery stalk in the bowl.
5. Then chopped the cooked chicken and add it in the arugula mixture.
6. In the shallow bowl, mix mustard with lemon juice, and mayonnaise.
7. Add the mixture in the salad and shake it well.

Nutrition Info:
- Per Serving: 184 calories, 21.7g protein, 7.1g carbohydrates, 7.5g fat, 1.3g fiber, 64mg cholesterol, 693mg sodium, 329mg potassium.

Goose And Sauce

Servings: 4
Cooking Time: 5 Hours
Ingredients:
- 1 goose breast half, skinless, boneless and cut into thin slices
- ¼ cup olive oil
- 1 sweet onion, chopped
- 2 teaspoons garlic, chopped
- Salt and black pepper to the taste
- ¼ cup sweet chili sauce

Directions:
1. In your Crock Pot, mix goose with oil, onion, garlic, salt, pepper and chili sauce, stir, cover and cook on Low for 5 hours.
2. Divide between plates and serve.

Nutrition Info:
- calories 192, fat 4, fiber 8, carbs 12, protein 22

Cilantro Chicken And Eggplant Mix

Servings: 2
Cooking Time: 7 Hours
Ingredients:
- 1 pound chicken breasts, skinless, boneless and sliced
- 2 eggplants, roughly cubed
- ½ cup chicken stock
- ½ cup tomato sauce
- 3 scallions, chopped
- A pinch of salt and black pepper
- 1 teaspoon chili powder
- 1 tablespoon cilantro, chopped

Directions:
1. In your Crock Pot, mix the chicken with the eggplant, stock and the other ingredients, toss, put the lid on, cook on Low for 7 hours, divide the mix between plates and serve.

Nutrition Info:
- calories 223, fat 9, fiber 2, carbs 4, protein 11

Lunch & Dinner Recipes

Lunch & Dinner Recipes

Stuffed Flank Steaks

Servings: 2
Cooking Time: 6 1/2 Hours
Ingredients:

- 2 thick flank steaks
- 1/2 cup grated Cheddar
- 1/4 cup cream cheese
- 1 red bell pepper, cored and diced
- Salt and pepper to taste
- 1/2 cup beef stock

Directions:

1. Mix the Cheddar with cream cheese, diced bell pepper, salt and pepper in a bowl.
2. Take each steak and make a small pocket into each one. Fill each steak with the cheese mix and secure the pocket with toothpicks.
3. Cover with a lid and place in your crock pot.
4. Add the stock and cook on low setting for 6 hours.
5. Serve the steaks warm with your favorite side dish.

Masala Beef Mix

Servings: 2
Cooking Time: 5 Hours
Ingredients:

- 1 pound beef roast meat, cubed
- 1 red onion, sliced
- 1 eggplant, cubed
- 2 tablespoons olive oil
- 1 teaspoon black mustard seeds
- A pinch of salt and black pepper
- 1 tablespoon lemon zest, grated
- 2 tablespoons lemon juice
- 1 tablespoon garam masala
- 1 tablespoons coriander powder
- 1 teaspoon turmeric powder
- ½ teaspoon black peppercorns, ground
- ½ cup beef stock

Directions:

1. In your Crock Pot, mix the meat with the onion, eggplant, oil, mustard seeds and the other ingredients, toss, put the lid on and cook on High for 5 hours.
2. Divide the mix between plates and serve for lunch with a side salad.

Nutrition Info:

- calories 300, fat 4, fiber 6, carbs 9, protein 22

Cheddar Pork Casserole

Servings: 6
Cooking Time: 5 1/2 Hours
Ingredients:

- 2 tablespoons canola oil
- 2 large onions, sliced
- 1 1/2 pounds ground pork
- 1 carrot, grated
- 1 cup finely chopped mushrooms
- 1/2 cup hot ketchup
- Salt and pepper to taste
- 2 cups grated Cheddar

Directions:

1. Heat the canola oil in a frying pan and add the onions. Cook on low heat for 10 minutes until they begin to caramelize.
2. Transfer the onions in your Crock Pot. Add the pork, carrot, mushrooms and ketchup and mix well, adjusting the taste with salt and pepper.
3. Top with Cheddar cheese and cook on low settings for 5 hours.
4. Serve the casserole preferably warm.

Bulgur Chili

Servings: 8
Cooking Time: 8 1/4 Hours
Ingredients:

- 1 cup bulgur wheat
- 1 large onion, chopped
- 2 cups sliced mushrooms
- 1 red bell pepper, cored and diced
- 2 garlic cloves, chopped
- 2 cups vegetable stock
- 1 cup diced tomatoes
- 1 can (15 oz.) black beans, drained
- 1 can (15 oz.) kidney beans, drained
- 1 tablespoon brown sugar
- 1 teaspoon apple cider vinegar
- 1 teaspoon chili powder
- Salt and pepper to taste
- 1 bay leaf
- 1 thyme sprig

Directions:

1. Combine the bulgur and the remaining ingredients in your crock pot.
2. Add salt and pepper to taste and cook on low settings for 8 hours, mixing a few times during the cooking time to make sure it's cooked evenly.
3. Serve the chili warm.

Honey Apple Pork Chops

Servings: 4
Cooking Time: 5 1/4 Hours
Ingredients:

- 4 pork chops
- 2 red, tart apples, peeled, cored and cubed
- 1 shallot, chopped
- 2 garlic cloves, chopped
- 1 tablespoon olive oil
- 1 red chili, chopped
- 1 heirloom tomato, peeled and diced
- 1 cup apple cider

- 2 tablespoons honey
- Salt and pepper to taste

Directions:
1. Mix all the ingredients in your crock pot.
2. Add salt and pepper to taste and cook on low settings for 5 hours.
3. Serve the chops warm and fresh.

Fennel Risotto

Servings: 6
Cooking Time: 4 1/4 Hours
Ingredients:
- 1 small fennel bulb, sliced
- 2 tablespoons olive oil
- 2 garlic cloves, chopped
- 1 shallot, chopped
- 1 cup white rice
- 1/4 cup white wine
- 2 cups vegetable stock
- Salt and pepper to taste

Directions:
1. Heat the oil in a skillet and add the garlic and shallot. Cook for 2 minutes until softened then stir in the fennel. Cook for another 2 minutes then transfer in your Crock Pot.
2. Add the remaining ingredients and season with salt and pepper.
3. Cook on low settings for 4 hours.
4. Serve the risotto warm and fresh.

Orange Marmalade Glazed Carrots

Servings: 4
Cooking Time: 4 1/4 Hours
Ingredients:
- 20 oz. baby carrots
- 1/4 cup orange marmalade
- 1/4 teaspoon chili powder
- 1 pinch nutmeg
- 2 tablespoons water
- 1/4 teaspoon cumin powder
- Salt and pepper to taste

Directions:
1. Combine the carrots and the remaining ingredients in your Crock Pot.
2. Add salt and pepper and cover with a lid.
3. Cook on low settings for 4 hours.
4. Serve the glazed carrots warm or chilled.

Sweet Potato And Clam Chowder

Servings: 2
Cooking Time: 3 Hours And 30 Minutes
Ingredients:

- 1 small yellow onion, chopped
- 1 carrot, chopped
- 1 red bell pepper, cubed
- 6 ounces canned clams, chopped

- 1 sweet potato, chopped
- 2 cups chicken stock
- ½ cup coconut milk
- 1 teaspoon Worcestershire sauce

Directions:

1. In your Crock Pot, mix the onion with the carrot, clams and the other ingredients, toss, put the lid on and cook on High for 3 hours.
2. Divide the chowder into bowls and serve for lunch.

Nutrition Info:

- calories 288, fat 15.3, fiber 5.9, carbs 36.4, protein 5

Bacon Potato Stew

Servings: 6
Cooking Time: 6 1/2 Hours
Ingredients:

- 1 cup diced bacon
- 1 large onion, chopped
- 2 carrots, diced
- 1 celery stalk, diced
- 2 red bell peppers, cored and diced
- 2 sweet potatoes, peeled and cubed

- 1 pound Yukon gold potatoes, peeled and cubed
- 1/2 teaspoon cumin seeds
- 1/2 teaspoon chili powder
- 1 cup diced tomatoes
- Salt and pepper to taste
- 2 cups chicken stock

Directions:

1. Heat a skillet and add the bacon. Cook until crisp then transfer in your Crock Pot.
2. Add the rest of the ingredients and adjust the taste with salt and pepper.
3. Cook on low settings for 6 hours.
4. Serve the stew warm and fresh.

Sweet Popcorn

Servings:4
Cooking Time: 20 Minutes
Ingredients:

- 2 cups popped popcorn
- 2 tablespoons butter

- 2 tablespoons brown sugar
- ½ teaspoon ground cinnamon

Directions:

1. Put butter and sugar in the Crock Pot.
2. Add ground cinnamon and cook the mixture on High or 15 minutes.

3. Then open the lid, stir the mixture, and add popped popcorn.
4. Carefully mix the ingredients with the help of the spatula and cook on high for 5 minutes more.

Nutrition Info:
- Per Serving: 84 calories, 0.6g protein, 7.8g carbohydrates, 5.9g fat, 0.7g fiber, 15mg cholesterol, 43mg sodium, 22mg potassium.

Lemon Chicken

Servings: 6
Cooking Time: 5 Hours
Ingredients:
- 6 chicken breast halves, skinless and bone in
- Salt and black pepper to the taste
- 1 teaspoon oregano, dried
- ¼ cup water
- 2 tablespoons butter
- 3 tablespoons lemon juice
- 2 garlic cloves, minced
- 1 teaspoon chicken bouillon granules
- 2 teaspoons parsley, chopped

Directions:
1. In your Crock Pot, mix chicken with salt, pepper, water, butter, lemon juice, garlic and chicken granules, stir, cover and cook on Low for 5 hours.
2. Add parsley, stir, divide between plates and serve for lunch.

Nutrition Info:
- calories 336, fat 10, fiber 1, carbs 1, protein 46

Crock Pot Ratatouille

Servings: 8
Cooking Time: 6 1/2 Hours
Ingredients:
- 1 large onion, chopped
- 1 tablespoon olive oil
- 4 garlic cloves, finely chopped
- 1 large zucchini, cubed
- 1 large eggplant, peeled and cubed
- 2 cups sliced mushrooms
- 3 ripe tomatoes, peeled and diced
- 2 red bell peppers, cored and diced
- 1/2 cup vegetable stock
- 1 thyme sprig
- Salt and pepper to taste

Directions:
1. Combine all the ingredients in your Crock Pot, adding salt and pepper as needed.
2. Cook on low settings for 6 hours.
3. The ratatouille can be served either warm or chilled.

Sweet Turkey

Servings: 12
Cooking Time: 3 Hours And 30 Minutes
Ingredients:

- 14 ounces chicken stock
- ¼ cup brown sugar
- ½ cup lemon juice
- ¼ cup lime juice
- ¼ cup sage, chopped
- ¼ cup cider vinegar
- 2 tablespoons mustard
- ¼ cup olive oil
- 1 tablespoon marjoram, chopped
- 1 teaspoon sweet paprika
- Salt and black pepper to the taste
- 1 teaspoon garlic powder
- 2 turkey breast halves, boneless and skinless

Directions:

1. In your blender, mix stock with brown sugar, lemon juice, lime juice, sage, vinegar, mustard, oil, marjoram, paprika, salt, pepper and garlic powder and pulse well.
2. Put turkey breast halves in a bowl, add blender mix, cover and leave aside in the fridge for 8 hours.
3. Transfer everything to your Crock Pot, cover and cook on High for 3 hours and 30 minutes.
4. Divide between plates and serve for lunch.

Nutrition Info:

- calories 219, fat 4, fiber 1, carbs 5, protein 36

Eggplant Parmigiana

Servings: 6
Cooking Time: 8 1/4 Hours
Ingredients:

- 4 medium eggplants, peeled and finely sliced
- 1/4 cup all-purpose flour
- 4 cups marinara sauce
- 1 cup grated Parmesan
- Salt and pepper to taste

Directions:

1. Season the eggplants with salt and pepper and sprinkle with flour.
2. Layer the eggplant slices and marinara sauce in your crock pot.
3. Top with the grated cheese and cook on low settings for 8 hours.
4. Serve the parmigiana warm or chilled.

Mushroom Stew

Servings: 2
Cooking Time: 6 Hours
Ingredients:

- 1 pound white mushrooms, sliced
- 2 carrots, peeled and cubed
- 1 red onion, chopped
- 1 tablespoon olive oil
- 1 tablespoon balsamic vinegar
- ½ cup tomato sauce
- Salt and black pepper to the taste
- 1 cup veggie stock

- 1 tablespoon basil, chopped

Directions:
1. In your Crock Pot, mix the mushrooms with the onion and the other ingredients, toss, put the lid on and cook on Low for 6 hours.
2. Divide the stew into bowls and serve.

Nutrition Info:
- calories 400, fat 15, fiber 4, carbs 25, protein 14

Chicken Dip

Servings:4
Cooking Time: 3.5 Hours
Ingredients:
- ½ cup white beans, canned, drained
- ½ cup ground chicken
- 1 teaspoon dried parsley
- ¼ cup BBQ sauce
- 1 teaspoon cayenne pepper
- ½ cup of water

Directions:
1. Blend the canned beans and transfer them in the Crock Pot.
2. Add ground chicken, dried parsley, BBQ sauce, cayenne pepper, and water.
3. Stir the ingredients and close the lid.
4. Cook the dip on High for 3.5 hours.

Nutrition Info:
- Per Serving: 142 calories, 11g protein, 21.2g carbohydrates, 1.6g fat, 4.1g fiber, 16mg cholesterol, 195mg sodium, 539mg potassium.

Sesame Glazed Chicken

Servings: 6
Cooking Time: 3 1/4 Hours
Ingredients:
- 6 chicken thighs
- 1 tablespoon sesame oil
- 2 tablespoon soy sauce
- 1 tablespoon brown sugar
- 2 tablespoons fresh orange juice
- 2 tablespoons hoisin sauce
- 1 teaspoon grated ginger
- 1 tablespoon cornstarch
- 2 tablespoons water
- 1 tablespoon sesame seeds

Directions:
1. Combine all the ingredients in your crock pot.
2. Cook the chicken on high settings for 3 hours.
3. Serve the chicken warm with your favorite side dish.

Soups & Stews Recipes

Soups & Stews Recipes

French Soup

Servings: 5
Cooking Time: 7 Hours
Ingredients:

- 5 oz Gruyere cheese, shredded
- 2 cups of water
- 2 cups chicken stock
- 2 cups white onion, diced
- ½ teaspoon cayenne pepper
- ½ cup heavy cream

Directions:

1. Pour chicken stock, water, and heavy cream in the Crock Pot.
2. Add onion, cayenne pepper, and close the lid.
3. Cook the ingredients on high for 4 hours.
4. When the time is finished, open the lid, stir the mixture, and add cheese.
5. Carefully mix the soup and cook it on Low for 3 hours.

Nutrition Info:

- Per Serving: 181 calories, 9.5g protein, 5.1g carbohydrates, 13.9g fat, 1g fiber, 48mg cholesterol, 410mg sodium, 110mg potassium.

Turmeric Squash Soup

Servings: 6
Cooking Time: 9 Hours
Ingredients:

- 3 chicken thighs, skinless, boneless, chopped
- 3 cups butternut squash, chopped
- 1 teaspoon ground turmeric
- 1 onion, sliced
- 1 oz green chilies, chopped, canned
- 6 cups of water

Directions:

1. Put chicken thighs in the bottom of the Crock Pot and top them with green chilies.
2. Then add the ground turmeric, butternut squash, and water.
3. Add sliced onion and close the lid.
4. Cook the soup on low for 9 Hours.

Nutrition Info:

- Per Serving: 194 calories, 22.6g protein, 13.4g carbohydrates, 5.8g fat, 3.2g fiber, 65mg cholesterol, 78mg sodium, 551mg potassium.

Lentil Stew

Servings:4
Cooking Time: 6 Hours
Ingredients:

- 2 cups chicken stock
- ½ cup red lentils
- 1 eggplant, chopped
- 1 tablespoon tomato paste
- 1 cup of water
- 1 teaspoon Italian seasonings

Directions:

1. Mix chicken stock with red lentils and tomato paste.
2. Pour the mixture in the Crock Pot.
3. Add eggplants and Italian seasonings.
4. Cook the stew on low for 6 hours.

Nutrition Info:

- Per Serving: 125 calories, 7.8g protein, 22.4g carbohydrates, 1.1g fat, 11.5g fiber, 1mg cholesterol, 392mg sodium, 540mg potassium.

Garlicky Spinach Soup With Herbed Croutons

Servings: 6
Cooking Time: 2 1/4 Hours
Ingredients:

- 1 pound fresh spinach, shredded
- 1/2 teaspoon dried oregano
- 1 shallot, chopped
- 4 garlic cloves, chopped
- 1/2 celery stalk, sliced
- 2 cups water
- 2 cups chicken stock
- Salt and pepper to taste
- 1 lemon, juiced
- 1/2 cup half and half
- 10 oz. one-day old bread, cubed
- 3 tablespoons olive oil
- 1 teaspoon dried basil
- 1 teaspoon dried marjoram

Directions:

1. Combine the spinach, oregano, shallot, garlic and celery in your Crock Pot.
2. Add the water, stock and lemon juice, as well as salt and pepper to taste and cook on high settings for 2 hours.
3. While the soup is cooking, place the bread cubes in a large baking tray and drizzle with olive oil. Sprinkle with salt and pepper and cook in the preheated oven at 375F for 10-12 minutes until crispy and golden.
4. When the soup is done, puree it with an immersion blender, adding the half and half while doing so.
5. Serve the soup warm, topped with herbed croutons.

Shrimp Chowder

Servings: 4
Cooking Time: 1 Hour
Ingredients:

- 1-pound shrimps
- ½ cup fennel bulb, chopped
- 1 bay leaf
- ½ teaspoon peppercorn
- 1 cup of coconut milk
- 3 cups of water
- 1 teaspoon ground coriander

Directions:

1. Put all ingredients in the Crock Pot.
2. Close the lid and cook the chowder on High for 1 hour.

Nutrition Info:

- Per Serving: 277 calories, 27.4g protein, 6.1g carbohydrates, 16.3g fat, 1.8g fiber, 239mg cholesterol, 297mg sodium, 401mg potassium.

Red Chili Quinoa Soup

Servings: 8
Cooking Time: 3 1/4 Hours
Ingredients:

- 2 shallots, chopped
- 1 carrot, diced
- 1/2 celery root, peeled and diced
- 1 can diced tomatoes
- 1/2 cup quinoa, rinsed
- 1 can (15 oz.) red beans, drained
- 2 cups water
- 2 cups chicken stock
- Salt and pepper to taste
- 1/2 teaspoon chili powder
- 2 tablespoons chopped cilantro for serving
- Sour cream for serving

Directions:

1. Combine the shallots, carrot, celery and diced tomatoes in your Crock Pot.
2. Add the quinoa, water, stock and chili powder and season with salt and pepper.
3. Cook on high settings for 3 hours.
4. Serve the soup warm, topped with cilantro and sour cream.

Quinoa Soup With Parmesan Topping

Servings: 6
Cooking Time: 3 1/2 Hours
Ingredients:

- 2 chicken breasts, cubed
- 2 tablespoons olive oil
- 2/3 cup quinoa, rinsed
- 1/2 teaspoon dried oregano
- 1/2 teaspoon dried basil
- 1 sweet onion, chopped
- 1 garlic clove, chopped
- 1 cup diced tomatoes
- 2 cups chicken stock
- 4 cups water
- Salt and pepper to taste
- 1 cup grated Parmesan for serving

Directions:

1. Heat the oil in a skillet and add the chicken. Cook on all sides until golden brown then transfer the chicken in your Crock Pot.
2. Add the remaining ingredients, except the Parmesan, and cook on high settings for 3 hours.
3. When done, pour the soup into serving bowls and top with grated Parmesan before serving.

Shrimp Soup

Servings: 6
Cooking Time: 6 1/4 Hours
Ingredients:

- 2 tablespoons olive oil
- 1 large sweet onion, chopped
- 1 fennel bulb, sliced
- 4 garlic cloves, chopped
- 1 cup dry white wine
- 1/2 cup tomato sauce
- 2 cup water
- 1 teaspoon dried oregano

- 1 teaspoon dried basil
- 1 pinch chili powder
- 4 medium size tomatoes, peeled and diced
- 1 bay leaf
- 1/2 pound cod fillets, cubed
- 1/2 pound fresh shrimps, peeled and deveined
- Salt and pepper to taste
- 1 lime, juiced

Directions:

1. Heat the oil in a skillet and stir in the onion, fennel and garlic. Sauté for 5 minutes until softened.
2. Transfer the mixture in your Crock Pot and stir in the wine, tomato sauce, water, oregano, basil, chili powder, tomatoes and bay leaf.
3. Cook on high settings for 1 hour then add the cod and shrimps, as well as lime juice, salt and pepper and continue cooking on low settings for 5 additional hours.
4. Serve the soup warm or chilled.

Ginger Fish Stew

Servings:5
Cooking Time: 6 Hours
Ingredients:

- 1 oz fresh ginger, peeled, chopped
- 1 cup baby carrot
- 1-pound salmon fillet, chopped
- 1 teaspoon fish sauce

- ½ teaspoon ground nutmeg
- ½ cup green peas
- 3 cups of water

Directions:

1. Put all ingredients in the Crock Pot bowl.
2. Gently stir the stew ingredients and close the lid.
3. Cook the stew on low for 6 hours.

Nutrition Info:

- Per Serving: 159 calories, 19.1g protein, 7.7g carbohydrates, 6.1g fat, 2g fiber, 40mg cholesterol, 153mg sodium, 506mg potassium.

Crock-pot Low-carb Taco Soup

Servings: 8
Cooking Time: 4 Hours
Ingredients:

- 2 lbs. ground pork, beef or sausage
- 2 8-ounce packages of cream cheese
- 2 10-ounce cans of Rotel
- 2 tablespoons of taco seasoning
- 4 cups chicken broth
- 2 tablespoons cilantro, fresh or dried
- 1 can corn kernels, drained
- ½ cup cheddar cheese, shredded for garnish (optional)

Directions:

1.   Brown the ground meat until fully cooked over medium-high heat in a pan. While the meat is browning, place cream cheese, Rotel, corn and taco seasoning in Crock-Pot. Drain grease off meat and place meat in Crock-Pot. Stir and combine. Pour chicken broth over mixture, cover and cook on LOW for 4 hours. Just before serving, add in cilantro and garnish with shredded cheddar cheese.

Nutrition Info:

- Calories: 547, Total Fat: 43 g, Saturated Fat: 20 g, Carbohydrates: 5 g, Sugar: 4 g Sodium: 1174 mg, Fiber: 1 g, Cholesterol: 168 mg, Protein: 33 g

Vegan Cream Of Tomato Soup

Servings: 4
Cooking Time: 3 Hours
Ingredients:

- 4 Roma tomatoes
- ½ cup sun dried tomatoes
- 1 teaspoon sea salt
- ¼ teaspoon black pepper
- ¼ teaspoon white pepper
- ¼ cup basil, fresh, chopped
- 1 clove of garlic
- 4 cups water

Directions:

1.   Add ingredients to a high-powered blender and blend until smooth, for about 5 minutes. Add the blended mix to Crock-Pot, cook on LOW for 3 hours. Serve hot.

Nutrition Info:

- Calories: 187, Total Fat: 15.9 g, Saturated Fat: 2.5 g, Sodium: 538 mg, Carbs: 11.8 g, Dietary Fiber: 4.1 g, Net Carbs: 7.7 g, Sugars: 3.4 g, Protein: 3.5 g

Chunky Mushroom Soup

Servings: 8
Cooking Time: 8 1/2 Hours
Ingredients:

- 1 sweet onion, chopped
- 1 garlic clove, chopped
- 1 yellow bell pepper, cored and diced
- 2 tablespoons olive oil
- 1 pound fresh mushrooms, chopped
- 1 zucchini, cubed

- 2 large potatoes, peeled and cubed
- 2 tomatoes, peeled and diced
- 2 cups vegetable stock
- 3 cups water
- 1/2 cup tomato sauce
- Salt and pepper to taste
- 1 lemon, juiced
- 1 tablespoon chopped dill

Directions:

1. Heat the oil in a skillet and stir in the onion, garlic and bell pepper. Sauté for 5 minutes until softened then transfer in your Crock Pot.
2. Add the mushrooms, zucchini, potatoes, tomatoes, stock, water and tomato sauce then season with salt and pepper.
3. Cook on low settings for 8 hours.
4. When done, add the lemon juice and chopped dill and serve the soup warm or chilled.

Beef Vegetable Soup

Servings: 8
Cooking Time: 7 1/4 Hours
Ingredients:

- 1 pound beef roast, cubed
- 2 tablespoons canola oil
- 1 celery stalk, sliced
- 1 sweet onion, chopped
- 1 carrot, sliced
- 1 garlic clove, chopped
- 1/2 head cauliflower, cut into florets
- 2 large potatoes, peeled and cubed
- 1 cup diced tomatoes
- 1/2 teaspoon dried basil
- 2 cups beef stock
- 4 cups water
- Salt and pepper to taste

Directions:

1. Heat the oil in a skillet and add the beef. Cook on all sides for a few minutes then transfer the beef in your Crock Pot.
2. Add the remaining ingredients and season with salt and pepper.
3. Cover and cook on low settings for 7 hours.
4. The soup is delicious either warm or chilled.

Chunky Potato Ham Soup

Servings: 8
Cooking Time: 8 1/2 Hours
Ingredients:

- 2 cups diced ham
- 1 sweet onion, chopped
- 1 garlic clove, chopped
- 1 leek, sliced
- 1 celery stalk, sliced
- 2 carrots, sliced
- 2 pounds potatoes, peeled and cubed
- 1/2 teaspoon dried oregano
- 1/2 teaspoon dried basil
- 2 cups chicken stock
- 3 cups water
- Salt and pepper to taste

Directions:

1. Combine all the ingredients in your Crock Pot.
2. Add salt and pepper to taste and cook on low settings for 8 hours.
3. Serve the soup warm or chilled.

Kielbasa Kale Soup

Servings: 8
Cooking Time: 6 1/4 Hours
Ingredients:

- 1 pound kielbasa sausages, sliced
- 1 sweet onion, chopped
- 1 carrot, diced
- 1 parsnip, diced
- 1 red bell pepper, cored and diced
- 1 can (15 oz.) white beans, drained
- 1 cup diced tomatoes
- 1/2 pound kale, shredded
- 2 cups chicken stock
- 2 cups water
- 1/2 teaspoon dried oregano
- 1/2 teaspoon dried basil
- Salt and pepper to taste

Directions:

1. Combine the kielbasa sausages, onion, carrot, parsnip, bell pepper, white beans, tomatoes and kale in a Crock Pot.
2. Add the remaining ingredients and season with salt and pepper.
3. Cook on low settings for 6 hours.
4. Serve the soup warm or chilled.

Sweet Corn Chowder

Servings: 8
Cooking Time: 6 1/4 Hours
Ingredients:

- 2 shallots, chopped
- 4 medium size potatoes, peeled and cubed1
- 1 celery stalk, sliced
- 1 can (15 oz.) sweet corn, drained
- 2 cups chicken stock
- 2 cups water
- Salt and pepper to taste

Directions:

1. Combine the shallot, potatoes, celery, corn, stock and water in a Crock Pot.
2. Add salt and pepper to taste and cook on low settings for 6 hours.
3. When done, remove a few tablespoons of corn from the pot then puree the remaining soup in the pot.
4. Pour the soup into serving bowls and top with the reserved corn.
5. Serve warm.

Moroccan Lamb Soup

Servings: 6
Cooking Time: 7 1/2 Hours
Ingredients:

- 1 pound lamb shoulder
- 1 teaspoon turmeric powder
- 1/2 teaspoon cumin powder
- 1/2 teaspoon chili powder
- 2 tablespoons canola oil
- 2 cups chicken stock
- 3 cups water

- 1 cup fire roasted tomatoes
- 1 cup canned chickpeas, drained
- 1 thyme sprig
- 1/2 teaspoon dried sage
- 1/2 teaspoon dried oregano
- Salt and pepper to taste
- 1 lemon, juiced

Directions:

1. Sprinkle the lamb with salt, pepper, turmeric, cumin powder and chili powder.
2. Heat the oil in a skillet and add the lamb. Cook on all sides for a few minutes then transfer it in a Crock Pot.
3. Add the remaining ingredients and season with salt and pepper.
4. Cook the soup on low settings for 7 hours.
5. Serve the soup warm.

Side Dish Recipes

Side Dish Recipes

Lemony Beets

Servings: 6
Cooking Time: 8 Hours
Ingredients:

- 6 beets, peeled and cut into medium wedges
- 2 tablespoons honey
- 2 tablespoons olive oil
- 2 tablespoons lemon juice
- Salt and black pepper to the taste
- 1 tablespoon white vinegar
- ½ teaspoon lemon peel, grated

Directions:

1. In your Crock Pot, mix beets with honey, oil, lemon juice, salt, pepper, vinegar and lemon peel, cover and cook on Low for 8 hours.
2. Divide between plates and serve as a side dish.

Nutrition Info:

- calories 80, fat 3, fiber 4, carbs 8, protein 4

Potatoes And Leeks Mix

Servings: 2
Cooking Time: 4 Hours
Ingredients:

- 2 leeks, sliced
- ½ pound sweet potatoes, cut into medium wedges
- ½ cup veggie stock
- ½ tablespoon balsamic vinegar
- 1 tablespoon chives, chopped
- ½ teaspoon pumpkin pie spice

Directions:

1. In your Crock Pot, mix the leeks with the potatoes and the other ingredients, toss, put the lid on and cook on High for 4 hours.
2. Divide between plates and serve as a side dish.

Nutrition Info:

- calories 351, fat 8, fiber 5, carbs 48, protein 7

Creamy Chipotle Sweet Potatoes

Servings: 10
Cooking Time: 4 Hours
Ingredients:

- 1 sweet onion, chopped
- 2 tablespoons olive oil
- ¼ cup parsley, chopped
- 2 shallots, chopped
- 2 teaspoons chipotle pepper, crushed
- Salt and black pepper
- 4 big sweet potatoes, shredded
- 8 ounces coconut cream
- 16 ounces bacon, cooked and chopped
- ½ teaspoon sweet paprika
- Cooking spray

Directions:

1. Heat up a pan with the oil over medium-high heat, add shallots and onion, stir, cook for 6 minutes and transfer to a bowl.
2. Add parsley, chipotle pepper, salt, pepper, sweet potatoes, coconut cream, paprika and bacon, stir, pour everything in your Crock Pot after you've greased it with some cooking spray, cover, cook on Low for 4 hours, leave aside to cool down a bit, divide between plates and serve as a side dish.

Nutrition Info:

- calories 260, fat 14, fiber 6, carbs 20, protein 15

Cauliflower And Potatoes Mix

Servings: 2
Cooking Time: 4 Hours
Ingredients:

- 1 cup cauliflower florets
- ½ pound sweet potatoes, peeled and cubed
- 1 cup veggie stock
- ½ cup tomato sauce
- 1 tablespoon chives, chopped
- Salt and black pepper to the taste
- 1 teaspoon sweet paprika

Directions:

1. In your Crock Pot, mix the cauliflower with the potatoes, stock and the other ingredients, toss, put the lid on and cook on High for 4 hours.
2. Divide between plates and serve as a side dish.

Nutrition Info:

- calories 135, fat 5, fiber 1, carbs 7, protein 3

Cumin Quinoa Pilaf

Servings: 2
Cooking Time: 2 Hours
Ingredients:

- 1 cup quinoa
- 2 teaspoons butter, melted
- Salt and black pepper to the taste
- 1 teaspoon turmeric powder

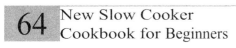

- 2 cups chicken stock
- 1 teaspoon cumin, ground

Directions:
1. Grease your Crock Pot with the butter, add the quinoa and the other ingredients, toss, put the lid on and cook on High for 2 hours
2. Divide between plates and serve as a side dish.

Nutrition Info:
- calories 152, fat 3, fiber 6, carbs 8, protein 4

Italian Black Beans Mix

Servings: 2
Cooking Time: 5 Hours
Ingredients:
- 2 tablespoons tomato paste
- Cooking spray
- 2 cups black beans
- ¼ cup veggie stock
- 1 red onion, sliced
- Cooking spray
- 1 teaspoon Italian seasoning
- ½ celery rib, chopped
- ½ red bell pepper, chopped
- ½ sweet red pepper, chopped
- ¼ teaspoon mustard seeds
- Salt and black pepper to the taste
- 2 ounces canned corn, drained
- 1 tablespoon cilantro, chopped

Directions:
1. Grease the Crock Pot with the cooking spray, and mix the beans with the stock, onion and the other ingredients inside.
2. Put the lid on, cook on Low for 5 hours, divide between plates and serve as a side dish.

Nutrition Info:
- calories 255, fat 6, fiber 7, carbs 38, protein 7

Asian Sesame Asparagus

Servings: 4
Cooking Time: 4 Hrs.
Ingredients:
- 1 tbsp sesame seeds
- 1 tsp miso paste
- ¼ cup of soy sauce
- 1 cup fish stock
- 8 oz. asparagus
- 1 tsp salt
- 1 tsp chili flakes
- 1 tsp oregano
- 1 cup of water

Directions:
1. Fill the insert of the Crock Pot with water and add asparagus.
2. Put the cooker's lid on and set the cooking time to 3 hours on High settings.
3. During this time, mix miso paste with soy sauce, fish stock, and sesame seeds in a suitable bowl.

4. Stir in oregano, chili flakes, and salt, then mix well.
5. Drain the slow-cooked asparagus then return it to the Crock Pot.
6. Pour the miso-stock mixture over the asparagus.
7. Put the cooker's lid on and set the cooking time to 1 hour on High settings.
8. Serve warm.

Nutrition Info:
- Per Serving: Calories: 85, Total Fat: 4.8g, Fiber: 2g, Total Carbs: 7.28g, Protein: 4g

White Beans Mix

Servings: 4
Cooking Time: 6 Hours
Ingredients:
- 1 celery stalk, chopped
- 2 garlic cloves, minced
- 1 carrot, chopped
- 1 cup veggie stock
- ½ cup canned tomatoes, crushed
- ½ teaspoon chili powder
- ½ tablespoon Italian seasoning
- 15 ounces canned white beans, drained
- 1 tablespoon parsley, chopped

Directions:
1. In your Crock Pot, mix the beans with the celery, garlic and the other ingredients, toss, put the lid on and cook on Low for 6 hours.
2. Divide the mix between plates and serve.

Nutrition Info:
- calories 223, fat 3, fiber 7, carbs 10, protein 7

Cauliflower Pilaf

Servings: 6
Cooking Time: 3 Hours
Ingredients:
- 1 cup cauliflower rice
- 6 green onions, chopped
- 3 tablespoons ghee, melted
- 2 garlic cloves, minced
- ½ pound Portobello mushrooms, sliced
- 2 cups warm water
- Salt and black pepper to the taste

Directions:
1. In your Crock Pot, mix cauliflower rice with green onions, melted ghee, garlic, mushrooms, water, salt and pepper, stir well, cover and cook on Low for 3 hours.
2. Divide between plates and serve as a side dish.

Nutrition Info:
- calories 200, fat 5, fiber 3, carbs 14, protein 4

Buttery Mushrooms

Servings: 6
Cooking Time: 4 Hours
Ingredients:

- 1 yellow onion, chopped
- 1 pounds mushrooms, halved
- ½ cup butter, melted
- 1 teaspoon Italian seasoning
- Salt and black pepper to the taste
- 1 teaspoon sweet paprika

Directions:

1. In your Crock Pot, mix mushrooms with onion, butter, Italian seasoning, salt, pepper and paprika, toss, cover and cook on Low for 4 hours.
2. Divide between plates and serve as a side dish.

Nutrition Info:

- calories 120, fat 6, fiber 1, carbs 8, protein 4

Classic Veggies Mix

Servings: 4
Cooking Time: 3 Hours
Ingredients:

- 1 and ½ cups red onion, cut into medium chunks
- 1 cup cherry tomatoes, halved
- 2 and ½ cups zucchini, sliced
- 2 cups yellow bell pepper, chopped
- 1 cup mushrooms, sliced
- 2 tablespoons basil, chopped
- 1 tablespoon thyme, chopped
- ½ cup olive oil
- ½ cup balsamic vinegar

Directions:

1. In your Crock Pot, mix onion pieces with tomatoes, zucchini, bell pepper, mushrooms, basil, thyme, oil and vinegar, toss to coat everything, cover and cook on High for 3 hours.
2. Divide between plates and serve as a side dish.

Nutrition Info:

- calories 150, fat 2, fiber 2, carbs 6, protein 5

Parmesan Rice

Servings: 2
Cooking Time: 2 Hours And 30 Minutes
Ingredients:

- 1 cup rice
- 2 cups chicken stock
- 1 tablespoon olive oil
- 1 red onion, chopped
- 1 tablespoon lemon juice
- Salt and black pepper to the taste
- 1 tablespoon parmesan, grated

Directions:

1. In your Crock Pot, mix the rice with the stock, oil and the other ingredients, toss, put the lid on and cook on High for 2 hours and 30 minutes.
2. Divide between plates and serve as a side dish.

Nutrition Info:

- calories 162, fat 4, fiber 6, carbs 29, protein 6

Farro Rice Pilaf

Servings: 12
Cooking Time: 5 Hours
Ingredients:

- 1 shallot, chopped
- 1 tsp garlic, minced
- A drizzle of olive oil
- 1 and ½ cups whole grain farro
- ¾ cup wild rice
- 6 cups chicken stock
- Salt and black pepper to the taste
- 1 tbsp parsley and sage, chopped
- ½ cup hazelnuts, toasted and chopped
- ¾ cup cherries, dried

Directions:

1. Add farro, rice, stock, and rest of the ingredients to the Crock Pot.
2. Put the cooker's lid on and set the cooking time to 5 hours on Low settings.
3. Serve warm.

Nutrition Info:

- Per Serving: Calories: 120, Total Fat: 2g, Fiber: 7g, Total Carbs: 20g, Protein: 3g

Lime Beans Mix

Servings: 2
Cooking Time: 8 Hours
Ingredients:

- ½ pound lima beans, soaked for 6 hours and drained
- 1 tablespoon olive oil
- 2 scallions, chopped
- 1 carrot, chopped
- 2 tablespoons tomato paste
- 1 garlic cloves, minced
- A pinch of salt and black pepper to the taste
- 3 cups water
- A pinch of red pepper, crushed
- 2 tablespoons parsley, chopped

Directions:

1. In your Crock Pot, mix the beans with the scallions, oil and the other ingredients, toss, put the lid on and cook on Low for 8 hours.
2. Divide between plates and serve as a side dish/

Nutrition Info:

- calories 160, fat 3, fiber 7, carbs 9, protein 12

Lemony Pumpkin Wedges

Servings: 4
Cooking Time: 6 Hours
Ingredients:

- 15 oz. pumpkin, peeled and cut into wedges
- 1 tbsp lemon juice
- 1 tsp salt
- 1 tsp honey
- ½ tsp ground cardamom
- 1 tsp lime juice

Directions:

1. Add pumpkin, lemon juice, honey, lime juice, cardamom, and salt to the Crock Pot.
2. Put the cooker's lid on and set the cooking time to 6 hours on Low settings.
3. Serve fresh.

Nutrition Info:

- Per Serving: Calories: 35, Total Fat: 0.1g, Fiber: 1g, Total Carbs: 8.91g, Protein: 1g

Cornbread Cream Pudding

Servings: 8
Cooking Time: 8 Hours
Ingredients:

- 11 oz. cornbread mix
- 1 cup corn kernels
- 3 cups heavy cream
- 1 cup sour cream
- 3 eggs
- 1 chili pepper
- 1 tsp salt
- 1 tsp ground black pepper
- 2 oz. pickled jalapeno
- ¼ tbsp sugar
- 1 tsp butter

Directions:

1. Whisk eggs in a suitable bowl and add cream and cornbread mix.
2. Mix it well then add salt, chili pepper, sour cream, sugar, butter, and black pepper.
3. Add corn kernels and pickled jalapeno then mix well to make a smooth dough.
4. Spread this dough in the insert of a Crock Pot.
5. Put the cooker's lid on and set the cooking time to 8 hours on Low settings.
6. Slice and serve.

Nutrition Info:

- Per Serving: Calories: 398, Total Fat: 27.9g, Fiber: 2g, Total Carbs: 29.74g, Protein: 9g

Saucy Macaroni

Servings: 6
Cooking Time: 3.5 Hours
Ingredients:

- 8 oz. macaroni
- 1 cup tomatoes, chopped
- 1 garlic clove, peeled
- 1 tsp butter
- 1 cup heavy cream

- 3 cups of water
- 1 tbsp salt
- 6 oz. Parmesan, shredded
- 1 tbsp dried basil

Directions:

1. Add macaroni, salt, and water to the Crock Pot.
2. Put the cooker's lid on and set the cooking time to 3 hours on High settings.
3. Meanwhile, puree tomatoes in a blender then add cheese, cream, butter, and dried basil.
4. Drain the cooked macaroni and return them to the Crock Pot.
5. Pour in the tomato-cream mixture.
6. Put the cooker's lid on and set the cooking time to 30 minutes on High settings.
7. Serve warm.

Nutrition Info:

- Per Serving: Calories: 325, Total Fat: 10.1g, Fiber: 2g, Total Carbs: 41.27g, Protein: 17g

Vegetable & Vegetarian Recipes

Vegetable & Vegetarian Recipes

Lemon Spinach Orzo

Servings: 5
Cooking Time: 2 Hrs 30 Minutes
Ingredients:

- 4 oz. shallot, chopped
- 7 oz. orzo
- 2 cup chicken stock
- 1 tsp paprika
- 1 tsp ground black pepper
- 1 tsp salt
- 1 lemon
- ¼ cup cream
- 2 yellow sweet pepper, chopped
- 1 cup baby spinach, chopped

Directions:

1. Add shallot, chicken stock, and paprika to the Crock Pot.
2. Drizzle salt, and black pepper in the cooker.
3. Put the cooker's lid on and set the cooking time to 30 minutes on High settings.
4. Now add spinach, sweet pepper, lemon zest and lemon juice, cream, and orzo to the shallot.
5. Put the cooker's lid on and set the cooking time to 2 hours on Low settings.
6. Serve warm.

Nutrition Info:

- Per Serving: Calories 152, Total Fat 4g, Fiber 3g, Total Carbs 24.79g, Protein 7g

Aromatic Marinated Mushrooms

Servings:4
Cooking Time: 5 Hours
Ingredients:

- 1 teaspoon dried rosemary
- 1 teaspoon dried thyme
- 1 teaspoon onion powder
- 2 cups of water
- 4 cups mushrooms, roughly chopped
- 1 teaspoon salt
- 1 teaspoon sugar
- ½ cup apple cider vinegar

Directions:

1. Pour water in the Crock Pot.
2. Add all remaining ingredients and carefully mix.
3. Cook the mushrooms on Low for 5 hours.
4. After this, transfer the mushrooms with liquid in the glass cans and cool well.
5. Store the mushrooms in the fridge for up to 4 days.

Nutrition Info :
- Per Serving: 29 calories, 2.3g protein, 4.4g carbohydrates, 0.3g fat, 1g fiber, 0mg cholesterol, 591mg sodium, 256mg potassium.

Potato Salad

Servings:2
Cooking Time: 3 Hours
Ingredients:
- 1 cup potato, chopped
- 1 cup of water
- 1 teaspoon salt
- 2 oz celery stalk, chopped
- 2 oz fresh parsley, chopped
- ¼ onion, diced
- 1 tablespoon mayonnaise

Directions:
1. Put the potatoes in the Crock Pot.
2. Add water and salt.
3. Cook the potatoes on High for 3 hours.
4. Then drain water and transfer the potatoes in the salad bowl.
5. Add all remaining ingredients and carefully mix the salad.

Nutrition Info :
- Per Serving: 129 calories, 5.5g protein, 12.4g carbohydrates, 6.7g fat, 2.5g fiber, 12mg cholesterol, 1479mg sodium, 465mg potassium.

Quinoa Fritters

Servings:4
Cooking Time: 1 Hour
Ingredients:
- 1 sweet potato, peeled, boiled, grated
- ½ cup quinoa, cooked
- 1 teaspoon chili powder
- 1 teaspoon salt
- 2 eggs, beaten
- 3 tablespoons cornflour
- 1 tablespoon coconut oil, melted

Directions:
1. In the mixing bowl mix grated sweet potato, quinoa, chili powder, salt, cornflour, and eggs.
2. Make the small fritters and put them in the Crock Pot.
3. Add coconut oil and close the lid.
4. Cook the fritters on High for 1 hour.

Nutrition Info:
- Per Serving: 187 calories, 6.8g protein, 24.3g carbohydrates, 7.3g fat, 3.1g fiber, 82mg cholesterol, 630mg sodium, 314mg potassium.

Cinnamon Banana Sandwiches

Servings: 4
Cooking Time: 2 Hrs
Ingredients:

- 2 bananas, peeled and sliced
- 8 oz. French toast slices, frozen
- 1 tbsp peanut butter
- ¼ tsp ground cinnamon
- 5 oz. Cheddar cheese, sliced
- ¼ tsp turmeric

Directions:

1. Layer half of the French toast slices with peanut butter.
2. Whisk cinnamon with turmeric and drizzle over the peanut butter layer.
3. Place the banana slice and cheese slices over the toasts.
4. Now place the remaining French toast slices on top.
5. Place these banana sandwiches in the Crock Pot.
6. Put the cooker's lid on and set the cooking time to 2 hours on High settings.
7. Serve.

Nutrition Info:

- Per Serving: Calories 248, Total Fat 7.5g, Fiber 2g, Total Carbs 36.74g, Protein 10g

Parmesan Scallops Potatoes

Servings:5
Cooking Time: 7 Hours
Ingredients:

- 5 potatoes
- 5 teaspoons vegan butter
- 1 teaspoon ground black pepper
- 1 teaspoon garlic powder
- 2 tablespoons flour
- 3 cups of milk
- 3 oz vegan Parmesan, grated

Directions:

1. Peel and slice the potatoes.
2. Then place the sliced potato in the Crock Pot in one layer.
3. Sprinkle the vegetables with ground black pepper, garlic powder, and butter.
4. After this, mix flour with milk and pour over the potatoes.
5. Then sprinkle the vegetables with Parmesan and close the lid.
6. Cook the meal on Low for 7 hours.

Nutrition Info:

- Per Serving: 323 calories, 14.4g protein, 44.3g carbohydrates, 10.7g fat, 5.4g fiber, 34mg cholesterol, 267mg sodium, 967mg potassium.

Cauliflower Curry

Servings:4
Cooking Time: 2 Hours
Ingredients:

- 4 cups cauliflower
- 1 tablespoon curry paste
- 2 cups of coconut milk

Directions:

1. In the mixing bowl mix coconut milk with curry paste until smooth.
2. Put cauliflower in the Crock Pot.
3. Pour the curry liquid over the cauliflower and close the lid.
4. Cook the meal on High for 2 hours.

Nutrition Info:

- Per Serving: 236 calories, 4.9g protein, 13g carbohydrates, 30.9g fat, 5.1g fiber, 0mg cholesterol, 48mg sodium, 619mg potassium.

Tarragon Pumpkin Bowl

Servings:2
Cooking Time: 4 Hours
Ingredients:

- 2 cups pumpkin, chopped
- 1 teaspoon dried tarragon
- 1 tablespoon coconut oil
- 1 cup of water
- 1 teaspoon salt

Directions:

1. Put all ingredients in the Crock Pot. Gently mix them.
2. Close the lid and cook pumpkin on High for 4 hours.

Nutrition Info:

- Per Serving: 143 calories, 2.8g protein, 20g carbohydrates, 7.5g fat, 7.1g fiber, 0mg cholesterol, 1179mg sodium, 515mg potassium.

Miso Asparagus

Servings:2
Cooking Time: 2.5 Hours
Ingredients:

- 1 teaspoon miso paste
- 1 cup of water
- 1 tablespoon fish sauce
- 10 oz asparagus, chopped
- 1 teaspoon avocado oil

Directions:

1. Mix miso paste with water and pour in the Crock Pot.

2. Add fish sauce, asparagus, and avocado oil.
3. Close the lid and cook the meal on High for 2.5 hours.

Nutrition Info:
• Per Serving: 40 calories, 3.9g protein, 6.7g carbohydrates, 0.6g fat, 3.2g fiber, 0mg cholesterol, 808mg sodium, 327mg potassium.

Eggplant Salad

Servings:5
Cooking Time: 3 Hours
Ingredients:
- 4 eggplants, cubed
- 1 teaspoon salt
- 1 teaspoon ground black pepper
- 1 cup of water
- 1 tablespoon sesame oil
- 1 tablespoon apple cider vinegar
- 1 teaspoon sesame seeds
- 2 cups tomatoes, chopped

Directions:
1. Mix eggplants with salt and ground black pepper and leave for 10 minutes.
2. Then transfer the eggplants in the Crock Pot. Add water and cook them for 3 hours on High.
3. Drain water and cool the eggplants to the room temperature.
4. Add sesame oil, apple cider vinegar, sesame seeds, and tomatoes.
5. Gently shake the salad.

Nutrition Info:
• Per Serving: 152 calories, 5.1g protein, 29g carbohydrates, 4g fat, 16.5g fiber, 0mg cholesterol, 479mg sodium, 1185mg potassium.

Split Pea Paste

Servings:4
Cooking Time: 2 Hours
Ingredients:
- 2 cups split peas
- 2 cups of water
- 1 tablespoon coconut oil
- 1 teaspoon salt
- 1 teaspoon ground black pepper

Directions:
1. Pour water in the Crock Pot.
2. Add split peas and close the lid.
3. Cook them for 2 hours on high or until they are soft.
4. Then drain water and transfer the split peas in the food processor.
5. Add coconut oil, salt, and ground black pepper.
6. Blend the mixture until smooth.

Nutrition Info:

- Per Serving: 367 calories, 24.2g protein, 59.8g carbohydrates, 4.6g fat, 25.3g fiber, 0mg cholesterol, 600mg sodium, 974mg potassium.

Ranch Broccoli

Servings:3
Cooking Time: 1.5 Hours
Ingredients:

- 3 cups broccoli
- 1 teaspoon chili flakes
- 2 tablespoons ranch dressing
- 2 cups of water

Directions:

1. Put the broccoli in the Crock Pot.
2. Add water and close the lid.
3. Cook the broccoli on high for 1.5 hours.
4. Then drain water and transfer the broccoli in the bowl.
5. Sprinkle it with chili flakes and ranch dressing. Shake the meal gently.

Nutrition Info:

- Per Serving: 34 calories, 2.7g protein, 6.6g carbohydrates, 0.3g fat, 2.4g fiber, 0mg cholesterol, 91mg sodium, 291mg potassium.

Zucchini Caviar

Servings:4
Cooking Time: 5 Hours
Ingredients:

- 4 cups zucchini, grated
- 2 onions, diced
- 2 tablespoons tomato paste
- 1 teaspoon salt
- 1 teaspoon ground black pepper
- 1 cup of water
- 1 teaspoon olive oil

Directions:

1. Put all ingredients in the Crock Pot.
2. Close the lid and cook the meal on Low for 5 hours.
3. Then carefully stir the caviar and cool it to the room temperature.

Nutrition Info:

- Per Serving: 58 calories, 2.4g protein, 10.8g carbohydrates, 1.5g fat, 2.9g fiber, 0mg cholesterol, 605mg sodium, 465mg potassium.

Chorizo Cashew Salad

Servings: 6
Cooking Time: 4 Hours 30 Minutes
Ingredients:

- 8 oz. chorizo, chopped
- 1 tsp olive oil
- 1 tsp cayenne pepper
- 1 tsp chili flakes
- 1 tsp ground black pepper
- 1 tsp onion powder
- 2 garlic cloves
- 3 tomatoes, chopped
- 1 cup lettuce, torn
- 1 cup fresh dill
- 1 tsp oregano
- 3 tbsp crushed cashews

Directions:

1. Add chorizo sausage to the Crock Pot.
2. Put the cooker's lid on and set the cooking time to 4 hours on High settings.
3. Mix chili flakes, cayenne pepper, black pepper, and onion powder in a bowl.
4. Now add tomatoes to the Crock Pot and cover again.
5. Crock Pot for another 30 minutes on High setting.
6. Stir in oregano and dill then mix well.
7. Add sliced garlic and torn lettuce to the mixture.
8. Garnish with cashews.
9. Serve.

Nutrition Info:

- Per Serving: Calories 249, Total Fat 19.8g, Fiber 2g, Total Carbs 7.69g, Protein 11g

Cream Zucchini Pasta

Servings:2
Cooking Time: 2 Hours
Ingredients:

- 2 large zucchinis, trimmed
- 1 cup coconut cream
- 1 teaspoon white pepper
- 2 oz vegan Parmesan, grated

Directions:

1. Make the strips from zucchini with the help of a spiralizer and put in the Crock Pot.
2. Add white pepper and coconut cream.
3. Then top the zucchini with grated vegan Parmesan and close the lid.
4. Cook the meal on low for 2 hours.

Nutrition Info:

- Per Serving: 223 calories, 14.1g protein, 16.3g carbohydrates, 13.4g fat, 3.8g fiber, 43mg cholesterol, 335mg sodium, 904mg potassium.

Cashew And Tofu Casserole

Servings: 4
Cooking Time: 3.5 Hours
Ingredients:

- 1 oz cashews, crushed
- 6 oz firm tofu, chopped
- 1 cup broccoli, chopped
- 1 red onion, sliced
- 1 tablespoon avocado oil
- ¼ cup of soy sauce
- ¼ cup maple syrup
- 1 tablespoon cornstarch
- ½ cup of water
- 1 teaspoon garlic powder

Directions:

1. Pour the avocado oil in the Crock Pot.
2. Then sprinkle the broccoli with garlic powder and put it in the Crock Pot.
3. Add cornstarch.
4. After this, add maple syrup, soy sauce, onion, and tofu.
5. Add cashews and water.
6. Close the lid and cook the casserole on Low for 3.5 hours.

Nutrition Info:

- Per Serving: 164 calories, 6.7g protein, 24g carbohydrates, 5.7g fat, 2.1g fiber, 0mg cholesterol, 917mg sodium, 309mg potassium.

Corn Pudding

Servings: 4
Cooking Time: 5 Hours
Ingredients:

- 3 cups corn kernels
- 2 cups heavy cream
- 3 tablespoons muffin mix
- 1 oz Parmesan, grated

Directions:

1. Mix heavy cream with muffin mix and pour the liquid in the Crock Pot.
2. Add corn kernels and Parmesan. Stir the mixture well.
3. Close the lid and cook the pudding on Low for 5 hours.

Nutrition Info:

- Per Serving: 371 calories, 21.8g protein, 31.4g carbohydrates, 26.3g fat, 3.2g fiber, 87mg cholesterol, 180mg sodium, 378mg potassium.

Snack Recipes

Snack Recipes

Jalapeno Onion Dip

Servings: 6
Cooking Time: 4 Hrs
Ingredients:

- 7 cups tomatoes, chopped
- 1 yellow onion, chopped
- 1 red onion, chopped
- 3 jalapenos, chopped
- 1 red bell pepper, chopped
- 1 green bell pepper, chopped
- ¼ cup apple cider vinegar
- 1 tbsp cilantro, chopped
- 1 tbsp sage, chopped
- 3 tbsp basil, chopped
- Salt to the taste

Directions:

1. Add tomatoes, onion and all other ingredients to the Crock Pot.
2. Put the cooker's lid on and set the cooking time to 4 hours on Low settings.
3. Puree the cooked mixture in a blender until smooth.
4. Serve.

Nutrition Info:
- Per Serving: Calories: 162, Total Fat: 7g, Fiber: 4g, Total Carbs: 7g, Protein: 3g

Beef And Chipotle Dip

Servings: 10
Cooking Time: 2 Hours
Ingredients:

- 8 ounces cream cheese, soft
- 2 tablespoons yellow onion, chopped
- 2 tablespoons mayonnaise
- 2 ounces hot pepper Monterey Jack cheese, shredded
- ¼ teaspoon garlic powder
- 2 chipotle chilies in adobo sauce, chopped
- 2 ounces dried beef, chopped
- ¼ cup pecans, chopped

Directions:

1. In your Crock Pot, mix cream cheese with onion, mayo, Monterey Jack cheese, garlic powder, chilies and dried beef, stir, cover and cook on Low for 2 hours.
2. Add pecans, stir, divide into bowls and serve.

Nutrition Info:
- calories 130, fat 11, fiber 1, carbs 3, protein 4

Nuts Bowls

Servings: 2
Cooking Time: 2 Hours
Ingredients:

- 2 tablespoons almonds, toasted
- 2 tablespoons pecans, halved and toasted
- 2 tablespoons hazelnuts, toasted and peeled
- 2 tablespoons sugar
- ½ cup coconut cream
- 2 tablespoons butter, melted
- A pinch of cinnamon powder
- A pinch of cayenne pepper

Directions:

1. In your Crock Pot, mix the nuts with the sugar and the other ingredients, toss, put the lid on, cook on Low for 2 hours, divide into bowls and serve as a snack.

Nutrition Info:

- calories 125, fat 3, fiber 2, carbs 5, protein 5

Peanut Bombs

Servings: 9
Cooking Time: 6 Hours
Ingredients:

- 1 cup peanut
- ½ cup flour
- 1 egg
- 1 tsp butter, melted
- 1 tsp salt
- 1 tsp turmeric
- 4 tbsp milk
- ¼ tsp nutmeg

Directions:

1. First, blend the peanuts in a blender then stir in flour.
2. Beat egg with milk, nutmeg, turmeric, and salt in a bowl.
3. Stir in the peanut-flour mixture and mix well to form a dough.
4. Grease the base of the Crock Pot with melted butter.
5. Divide the dough into golf ball-sized balls and place them the cooker.
6. Put the cooker's lid on and set the cooking time to 6 hours on Low settings.
7. Serve.

Nutrition Info:

- Per Serving: Calories: 215, Total Fat: 12.7g, Fiber: 2g, Total Carbs: 17.4g, Protein: 10g

Chickpeas Salsa

Servings: 2
Cooking Time: 6 Hours
Ingredients:

- 1 cup canned chickpeas, drained
- 1 cup veggie stock
- ½ cup black olives, pitted and halved
- 1 small yellow onion, chopped
- ¼ tablespoon ginger, grated
- 4 garlic cloves, minced
- ¼ tablespoons coriander, ground
- ¼ tablespoons red chili powder
- ¼ tablespoons garam masala
- 1 tablespoon lemon juice

Directions:

1. In your Crock Pot, mix the chickpeas with the stock, olives and the other ingredients, toss, put the lid on and cook on Low for 6 hours.
2. Divide into bowls and serve as an appetizer.

Nutrition Info:
- calories 355, fat 5, fiber 14, carbs 16, protein 11

Eggplant Dip

Servings: 4
Cooking Time: 4 Hours And 10 Minutes
Ingredients:

- 1 eggplant
- 1 zucchini, chopped
- 2 tablespoons olive oil
- 2 tablespoons balsamic vinegar
- 1 tablespoon parsley, chopped
- 1 yellow onion, chopped
- 1 celery stick, chopped
- 1 tomato, chopped
- 2 tablespoons tomato paste
- 1 and ½ teaspoons garlic, minced
- A pinch of sea salt
- Black pepper to the taste

Directions:

1. Brush eggplant with the oil, place on preheated grill and cook over medium-high heat for 5 minutes on each side.
2. Leave aside to cool down, chop it and put in your Crock Pot.
3. Also add, zucchini, vinegar, onion, celery, tomato, parsley, tomato paste, garlic, salt and pepper and stir everything.
4. Cover and cook on High for 4 hours.
5. Stir your spread again very well, divide into bowls and serve.

Nutrition Info:
- calories 110, fat 1, fiber 2, carbs 7, protein 5

Sugary Chicken Wings

Servings: 24
Cooking Time: 6 Hours
Ingredients:

- 1 teaspoon garlic powder
- ½ cup brown sugar
- ¾ cup white sugar
- 1 teaspoon ginger powder
- 1 cup soy sauce
- ¼ cup pineapple juice
- ¾ cup water
- ¼ cup olive oil
- 24 chicken wings

Directions:

1. In a bowl, mix chicken wings with garlic powder, brown sugar, white sugar, ginger powder, soy sauce, pineapple juice, water and oil, whisk well and leave aside for 2 hours in the fridge.

2. Transfer chicken wings to your Crock Pot, add 1 cup of the marinade, cover and cook on Low for 6 hours.
3. Serve chicken wings warm.

Nutrition Info:
*   calories 140, fat 7, fiber 1, carbs 12, protein 6

Crab Dip(2)

Servings: 6
Cooking Time: 2 Hours
Ingredients:
*   12 ounces cream cheese
*   ½ cup parmesan, grated
*   ½ cup mayonnaise
*   ½ cup green onions, chopped
*   2 garlic cloves, minced
*   Juice of 1 lemon
*   1 and ½ tablespoon Worcestershire sauce
*   1 and ½ teaspoons old bay seasoning
*   12 ounces crabmeat

Directions:
1. In your Crock Pot, mix cream cheese with parmesan, mayo, green onions, garlic, lemon juice, Worcestershire sauce, old bay seasoning and crabmeat, stir, cover and cook on Low for 2 hours.
2. Divide into bowls and serve as a dip.

Nutrition Info:
*   calories 200, fat 4, fiber 6, carbs 12, protein 3

Spicy Dip

Servings: 10
Cooking Time: 3 Hours
Ingredients:
*   1 pound spicy sausage, chopped
*   8 ounces cream cheese, soft
*   8 ounces sour cream
*   20 ounces canned tomatoes and green chilies, chopped

Directions:
1. In your Crock Pot, mix sausage with cream cheese, sour cream and tomatoes and chilies, stir, cover and cook on Low for 3 hours.
2. Divide into bowls and serve as a snack.

Nutrition Info:
*   calories 300, fat 12, fiber 7, carbs 30, protein 34

Caramel Milk Dip

Servings: 4
Cooking Time: 2 Hours
Ingredients:

- 1 cup butter
- 12 oz. condensed milk
- 2 cups brown sugar
- 1 cup of corn syrup

Directions:

1. Add butter, milk, corn syrup, and sugar to the Crock Pot.
2. Put the cooker's lid on and set the cooking time to 2 hours on High settings.
3. Serve warm.

Nutrition Info:

- Per Serving: Calories: 172, Total Fat: 2g, Fiber: 6g, Total Carbs: 12g, Protein: 4g

Spaghetti Squash

Servings: 6 (6.8 Ounces)
Cooking Time: 6 Hours
Ingredients:

- 1 spaghetti squash (vegetable spaghetti)
- 4 tablespoon olive oil
- 1 ¾ cups water
- Sea salt

Directions:

1. Slice the squash in half lengthwise and scoop out the seeds. Drizzle the halves with olive oil and season with sea salt. Place the squash in Crock-Pot and add the water. Close the lid and cook on LOW for 4-6 hours. Remove the squash and allow it to cool for about 30 minutes. Use a fork to scrape out spaghetti squash.

Nutrition Info:

- Calories: 130.59, Total Fat: 9.11 g, Saturated Fat: 1.27 g, Cholesterol: 0 mg, Sodium: 6.79 mg, Potassium: 399.95 mg, Total Carbohydrates: 13.26 g, Fiber: 2.27 g, Sugar: 2.49 g, Protein: 1.13 g

Curry Pork Meatballs

Servings: 2
Cooking Time: 4 Hours
Ingredients:

- ½ pound pork stew meat, ground
- 1 red onion, chopped
- 1 egg, whisked
- Salt and black pepper to the taste
- 1 tablespoon cilantro, chopped
- 5 ounces coconut milk
- ¼ tablespoon green curry paste

Directions:

1. In a bowl, mix the meat with the onion and the other ingredients except the coconut milk, stir well and shape medium meatballs out of this mix.

2. Put the meatballs in your Crock Pot, add the coconut milk, put the lid on and cook on High for 4 hours.
3. Arrange the meatballs on a platter and serve them as an appetizer

Nutrition Info:
- calories 225, fat 6, fiber 2, carbs 8, protein 4

Apple Jelly Sausage Snack

Servings: 15
Cooking Time: 2 Hours
Ingredients:
- 2 pounds sausages, sliced
- 18 ounces apple jelly
- 9 ounces Dijon mustard

Directions:
1. Place sausage slices in your Crock Pot, add apple jelly and mustard, toss to coat well, cover and cook on Low for 2 hours.
2. Divide into bowls and serve as a snack.

Nutrition Info:
- calories 200, fat 3, fiber 1, carbs 9, protein 10

Apple And Carrot Dip

Servings: 2
Cooking Time: 6 Hours
Ingredients:
- 2 cups apples, peeled, cored and chopped
- 1 cup carrots, peeled and grated
- ¼ teaspoon cloves, ground
- ¼ teaspoon ginger powder
- 1 tablespoon lemon juice
- ½ tablespoon lemon zest, grated
- ½ cup coconut cream
- ¼ teaspoon nutmeg, ground

Directions:
1. In your Crock Pot, mix the apples with the carrots, cloves and the other ingredients, toss, put the lid on and cook on Low for 6 hours.
2. Bend using an immersion blender, divide into bowls and serve.

Nutrition Info:
- calories 212, fat 4, fiber 6, carbs 12, protein 3

Mozzarella Basil Tomatoes

Servings: 8
Cooking Time: 30 Minutes
Ingredients:

- 3 tbsp fresh basil
- 1 tsp chili flakes
- 5 oz. Mozzarella, sliced
- 4 large tomatoes, sliced
- 1 tbsp olive oil
- 1 tsp minced garlic
- ½ tsp onion powder
- ½ tsp cilantro

Directions:

1. Whisk olive oil with onion powder, cilantro, garlic, and chili flakes in a bowl.
2. Rub all the tomato slices with this cilantro mixture.
3. Top each tomato slice with cheese slice and then place another tomato slice on top to make a sandwich.
4. Insert a toothpick into each tomato sandwich to seal it.
5. Place them in the base of the Crock Pot.
6. Put the cooker's lid on and set the cooking time to 20 minutes on High settings.
7. Garnish with basil.
8. Enjoy.

Nutrition Info:

- Per Serving: Calories: 59, Total Fat: 1.9g, Fiber: 2g, Total Carbs: 4.59g, Protein: 7g

Almond Bowls

Servings: 2
Cooking Time: 4 Hours
Ingredients:

- 1 tablespoon cinnamon powder
- 1 cup sugar
- 2 cups almonds
- ½ cup water
- ½ teaspoons vanilla extract

Directions:

1. In your Crock Pot, mix the almonds with the cinnamon and the other ingredients, toss, put the lid on and cook on Low for 4 hours.
2. Divide into bowls and serve as a snack.

Nutrition Info:

- calories 260, fat 3, fiber 4, carbs 12, protein 8

Fajita Dip

Servings: 6
Cooking Time: 4 Hours
Ingredients:

- 3 chicken breasts, skinless and boneless
- 8 ounces root beer
- 3 red bell peppers, chopped
- 1 yellow onion, chopped
- 8 ounces cream cheese
- 8 ounces pepper jack cheese, shredded
- 16 ounces sour cream
- 2 fajita seasoning mix packets
- 1 tablespoons olive oil
- Salt and black pepper to the taste

Directions:

1. In your Crock Pot, mix chicken with root beer, bell peppers, onion, cream cheese, pepper jack cheese, sour cream, fajita seasoning, oil, salt and pepper, stir, cover and cook on High for 4 hours.
2. Shred meat using 2 forks, divide into bowls and serve.

Nutrition Info:

- calories 261, fat 4, fiber 6, carbs 17, protein 5

Dessert Recipes

Dessert Recipes

Lemon Berry Cake

Servings: 10
Cooking Time: 4 1/2 Hours
Ingredients:

- 1 cup butter, softened
- 1 cup white sugar
- 1 teaspoon vanilla extract
- 2 teaspoons lemon zest
- 4 eggs
- 1 cup all-purpose flour
- 1 teaspoon baking powder
- 1/4 teaspoon salt
- 1 cup fresh mixed berries

Directions:

1. Mix the butter, sugar and vanilla in a bowl until creamy.
2. Add the eggs, one by one, as well as the lemon zest and mix for 1 minute on high speed.
3. Fold in the flour, baking powder and salt then spoon the batter in your Crock Pot.
4. Cover the pot and cook for 4 hours on low settings.
5. Allow the cake to cool before serving.

Spiced Poached Pears

Servings: 6
Cooking Time: 6 1/2 Hours
Ingredients:

- 6 ripe but firm pears
- 2 cups white wine
- 1 1/2 cups water
- 3/4 cup white sugar
- 1 star anise
- 1-inch piece of ginger, sliced
- 4 whole cloves
- 2 cinnamon stick
- 2 cardamom pods, crushed

Directions:

1. Carefully peel and core the pears and place them in your crock pot.
2. Add the remaining ingredients and cook on low settings for 6 hours.
3. The pears are best served chilled.

Dark Chocolate Cream

Servings: 6
Cooking Time: 1 Hour
Ingredients:

- ½ cup heavy cream
- 4 ounces dark chocolate, unsweetened and chopped

Directions:

1. In your Crock Pot, mix cream with chocolate, stir, cover, cook on High for 1 hour, divide into bowls and serve cold.

Nutrition Info:

- calories 78, fat 1, fiber 1, carbs 2, protein 1

Wine Dipped Pears

Servings: 6
Cooking Time: 1 Hr. 30 Minutes
Ingredients:

- 6 green pears
- 1 vanilla pod
- 1 clove
- A pinch of cinnamon
- 7 oz. sugar
- 1 glass red wine

Directions:

1. Add pears, cinnamon, vanilla, wine, cloves, and sugar to the insert of Crock Pot.
2. Put the cooker's lid on and set the cooking time to 1.5 hours on High settings.
3. Serve the pears with wine sauce.

Nutrition Info:

- Per Serving: Calories: 162, Total Fat: 4g, Fiber: 3g, Total Carbs: 6g, Protein: 3g

Overnight Plum Pudding

Servings: 8
Cooking Time: 8 1/4 Hours
Ingredients:

- 1 1/2 cups all-purpose flour
- 1/4 cup dark brown sugar
- 1/2 teaspoon baking soda
- 4 tablespoons butter, softened
- 2 eggs
- 1 cup mixed dried fruits, chopped
- 1/2 cup dried plums, chopped
- 1 cup hot water

Directions:

1. Mix the dried fruits, plums and hot water in a bowl and allow to soak up for 10 minutes.
2. Combine the flour, brown sugar, baking soda, butter, eggs and the dried fruits plus the water in a large bowl.
3. Mix well with a spoon or spatula then spoon the batter in your crock pot.
4. Cover and cook on low settings for 8 hours.
5. Allow the pudding to cool in the pot before serving.

Banana Cake

Servings: 6
Cooking Time: 2 Hours
Ingredients:

- ¾ cup sugar
- 1/3 cup butter, soft
- 1 teaspoon vanilla
- 1 egg
- 3 bananas, mashed
- 1 teaspoon baking powder
- 1 and ½ cups flour
- ½ teaspoons baking soda
- 1/3 cup milk
- Cooking spray

Directions:

1. In a bowl, mix butter with sugar, vanilla extract, eggs, bananas, baking powder, flour, baking soda and milk and whisk.
2. Grease your Crock Pot with the cooking spray, add the batter, spread, cover and cook on High for 2 hours.
3. Leave the cake to cool down, slice and serve.

Nutrition Info:

- calories 300, fat 4, fiber 4, carbs 27, protein 4

Chocolate Pudding

Servings: 4
Cooking Time: 1 Hour
Ingredients:

- 4 ounces heavy cream
- 4 ounces dark chocolate, cut into chunks
- 1 teaspoon sugar

Directions:

1. In a bowl, mix the cream with chocolate and sugar, whisk well, pour into your Crock Pot, cover and cook on High for 1 hour.
2. Divide into bowls and serve cold.

Nutrition Info:

- calories 232, fat 12, fiber 6, carbs 9, protein 4

Berry Cream

Servings: 2
Cooking Time: 2 Hours
Ingredients:

- 2 tablespoons cashews, chopped
- 1 cup heavy cream
- ½ cup blueberries
- ½ cup maple syrup
- ½ tablespoon coconut oil, melted

Directions:

1. In your Crock Pot, mix the cream with the berries and the other ingredients, whisk, put the lid on and cook on Low for 2 hours.
2. Divide the mix into bowls and serve cold.

Nutrition Info:
- calories 200, fat 3, fiber 5, carbs 12, protein 3

Dump Cake

Servings:8
Cooking Time: 5 Hours
Ingredients:
- 1 cupcake mix
- 1 teaspoon vanilla extract
- ½ teaspoon ground nutmeg
- 1 tablespoon butter, melted
- 2 eggs, beaten
- 1 teaspoon lemon zest, grated
- ½ cup heavy cream
- 4 pecans, chopped

Directions:
1. In the bowl mix all ingredients except pecans.
2. The line the Crock Pot with baking paper and pour the dough inside.
3. Flatten the batter and top with pecans.
4. Close the lid and cook the dump cake for 5 hours on Low.
5. Cook the cooked cake well before serving.

Nutrition Info:
- Per Serving: 245 calories, 3.8g protein, 27g carbohydrates, 13.9g fat, 1.1g fiber, 55mg cholesterol, 246mg sodium, 90mg potassium

Lentil Pudding

Servings:4
Cooking Time: 6 Hours
Ingredients:
- ½ cup green lentils
- 3 cups of milk
- 2 tablespoons of liquid honey
- 1 teaspoon vanilla extract
- 1 teaspoon cornflour

Directions:
1. Put all ingredients in the Crock Pot and carefully mix.
2. Close the lid and cook the pudding on Low for 6 hours.
3. Cool the pudding to the room temperature and transfer in the serving bowls.

Nutrition Info:
- Per Serving: 213 calories, 12.3g protein, 32.7g carbohydrates, 4g fat, 7.4g fiber, 15mg cholesterol, 88mg sodium, 343mg potassium.

Cardamom Coconut Rice Pudding

Servings: 6
Cooking Time: 6 1/4 Hours
Ingredients:

- 1 1/4 cups Arborio rice
- 2 cups coconut milk
- 1 cup coconut water
- 1/2 cup coconut sugar
- 4 cardamom pods, crushed
- Sliced peaches for serving

Directions:

1. Combine all the ingredients in your crock pot.
2. Cover the pot and cook on low settings for 6 hours.
3. The pudding is best served warm, although it tastes good chilled as well. For more flavor, top the pudding with sliced peaches just before serving.

Vanilla Pears

Servings: 2
Cooking Time: 2 Hours
Ingredients:

- 2 tablespoons avocado oil
- 1 teaspoon vanilla extract
- 2 pears, cored and halved
- ½ tablespoon lime juice
- 1 tablespoon sugar

Directions:

1. In your Crock Pot combine the pears with the sugar, oil and the other ingredients, toss, put the lid on and cook on High for 2 hours.
2. Divide between plates and serve.

Nutrition Info:

- calories 200, fat 4, fiber 6, carbs 16, protein 3

Vanilla Bean Caramel Custard

Servings: 6
Cooking Time: 6 1/4 Hours
Ingredients:

- 1 cup white sugar for melting
- 4 cups whole milk
- 1 cup heavy cream
- 2 egg yolks
- 4 eggs
- 1 tablespoon vanilla bean paste
- 2 tablespoons white sugar

Directions:

1. Caramelize 1 cup of sugar in a thick saucepan until it has an amber color. Pour the caramel in your Crock Pot and swirl to coat the bottom and sides as much as possible.
2. Mix the milk, cream, egg yolks, eggs, vanilla bean paste and sugar in a bowl. Pour this mixture over the caramel.

3. Cover the pot and cook on low settings for 6 hours.
4. Serve the custard chilled.

Rhubarb Stew

Servings: 2
Cooking Time: 2 Hours
Ingredients:

- ½ pound rhubarb, roughly sliced
- 2 tablespoons sugar
- ½ teaspoon vanilla extract
- ½ teaspoon lemon extract
- 1 tablespoon lemon juice
- ¼ cup water

Directions:
1. In your Crock Pot, mix the rhubarb with the sugar, vanilla and the other ingredients, toss, put the lid on and cook on Low for 2 hours.
2. Divide the mix into bowls and serve cold.

Nutrition Info:
- calories 60, fat 1, fiber 0, carbs 10, protein 1

Green Tea Avocado Pudding

Servings: 2
Cooking Time: 1 Hr.
Ingredients:

- ½ cup of coconut milk
- 1 and ½cup avocado, pitted and peeled
- 2 tbsp green tea powder
- 2 tsp lime zest, grated
- 1 tbsp sugar

Directions:
1. Mix coconut milk with tea powder and rest of the ingredients in the insert of Crock Pot.
2. Put the cooker's lid on and set the cooking time to 1 hour on Low settings.
3. Divide the pudding into the serving cups and allow it to cool.
4. Serve.

Nutrition Info:
- Per Serving: Calories: 107, Total Fat: 5g, Fiber: 3g, Total Carbs: 6g, Protein: 8g

Apricot And Peaches Cream

Servings: 2
Cooking Time: 2 Hours
Ingredients:

- 1 cup apricots, pitted and chopped
- 1 cup peaches, pitted and chopped
- 1 cup heavy cream
- 3 tablespoons brown sugar
- 1 teaspoon vanilla extract

Directions:

1. In a blender, mix the apricots with the peaches and the other ingredients, and pulse well.
2. Put the cream in the Crock Pot, put the lid on, cook on High for 2 hours, divide into bowls and serve.

Nutrition Info:

- calories 200, fat 4, fiber 5, carbs 10, protein 4

Apple Cherry Cobbler

Servings: 10
Cooking Time: 4 1/2 Hours
Ingredients:

- 1 pound cherries, pitted
- 4 red apples, peeled and sliced
- 4 tablespoons maple syrup
- 2 tablespoons cornstarch
- 1 tablespoon lemon juice
- 1 1/4 cups all-purpose flour
- 1/2 cup butter, chilled and cubed
- 2 tablespoons white sugar
- 1/2 cup buttermilk, chilled

Directions:

1. Combine the cherries, apples, maple syrup, cornstarch and lemon juice in your crock pot.
2. For the topping, mix the flour, butter and sugar in a bowl and rub the mix well with your fingertips until grainy.
3. Stir in the buttermilk and give it a quick mix.
4. Spoon the batter over the fruit mixture and bake on low settings for 4 hours.
5. Serve the cobbler chilled.

Appendix:Recipes Index

Printed in Great Britain
by Amazon